POSITIVE AFFIRMATIONS FOR BLACK WOMEN

Table of Contents:

Introduction

It's been stated that what you think becomes what you say, and what you say becomes what you do. What you say to yourself every day, whether you realize it or not, is either powerful or disempowering. The question is, which one would you prefer?

Positive affirmations for black women serve as a reminder of your own strength, intelligence, and authority. These are also reminders of the inner and outer beauty that black women possess. It's no surprise that these chants are essential for black women because self-hatred can often be found in the narrative, we tell ourselves about who we are as people - especially when it comes to feminism in general.

There is a long history of oppression and disempowerment for black women, but that does not mean we have to accept it as our new reality. The fact that the status quo has been established over time does not make it true. Every person on this planet has the power to make a positive difference.

The truth is that we are disempowered in certain areas yet empowered in others. We have the option of choosing which one we wish to be. It's no different than being a man: when men were denied equal rights, many of them were forced to live under oppression they didn't like.

There was no way to change the dynamic until the guys who felt this way resolved to establish a movement to take back control of their lives. They didn't allow society to convince them that wanting more was wrong, or that wanting respect was wrong. When it comes to positive affirmations for black women, the ongoing disempowerment of men and women equally is still an issue in modern times.

Affirmations that assist you to realize what you are capable of are necessary for self-empowerment. You'll need a mantra to assist you break free from the negative story that's running through your thoughts. These affirmations for black women can help you concentrate on the positive aspects of your life.

You don't have to disregard the reality that black women are more prone than white women to have health problems like breast cancer or diabetes, but you should constantly remember that this is not a given. Proper eating and exercise can help to prevent certain health problems. That's something to be proud of!

Affirmations don't have to be novel or fancy to be effective; they simply have to match with what makes sense and is true for you. You might want to consider making a list of these affirmation kinds so that you can easily refer back to it whenever you need a reminder.

You may write something like "I am powerful" or "I am gorgeous," for example. Remember that each woman is unique and will have her own set of affirmations for black women. We all have different needs, but don't worry - there are lots of resources here to help you get started on your path to empowerment!

Importance of Positive Affirmation

It triggers the circuits in your brain that control arousal and motivation when you feed yourself with positive self-statements. Your drive and desire to accomplish your best work rise as a result of motivation. It provides you a sense of direction, autonomy, and mastery. By strengthening mental toughness and increasing your ability to focus, motivation increases your desire to achieve your goals. When you're focused, you'll begin working on your goal, and your drive to achieve your objectives will grow. Motivation instills confidence and allows you to mentally prepare. This is necessary in order to win in challenging situations. Motivation will assist you in increasing or maintaining the amount of work you put in to achieve your objectives.

Your attention will be drawn to your goal if you repeat your affirmations. Goal attainment is aided by focusing your thoughts on the intended outcome. Affirmations are designed to draw your attention away from disappointments or flaws. They focus your attention on the qualities you already have and those you need to develop. Without focus, it's easy to lose sight of how to reach one's full potential. Positive affirmations will make it easier for you to focus your efforts and time on your goals. You'll be able to choose where you want to focus your attention, making it easier to devote your time and energy to it. If you wish to be an entrepreneur, for example, this will be a major priority in your life.

Affirmations will assist you gain confidence in yourself and your ability to achieve your objectives. As you practice them, you'll feel more confident in yourself. You will be more successful in your endeavors if you are confident. As a result, your self-assurance will rise. This is a happy cycle that leads to success and happiness. To get the most out of these statements, you'll have to act on them on a daily basis. You can persuade yourself that you are now confident through practice. These affirmations can help you think about how to reach your objectives.

Positive affirmations must be repeated on a daily basis to improve self-efficacy. Self-efficacy is the belief in one's ability to arrange and carry out the game plans necessary to achieve a specific outcome. As a result, making positive affirmations a habit will serve to reinforce the views you've established as a result of achieving a goal. When you have a high level of self-efficacy, you'll be able to:

Consider challenging problems as challenges to conquer.

Construct a more solid sense of dedication to your hobbies and activities.

Continually pique your interest in the activities you appreciate.

Recover from your setbacks and disappointments.

Racial and Self-Affirmations

Being a woman is difficult enough, but being a black woman in a world where dark skin is considered unattractive is even more difficult. We are subjected to prejudice and other unfavorable circumstances as a result of our race. It's past time for us to start protecting our minds and bodies from the harsh truths of life.

Because of racism and discrimination, I, too, suffered with my self-esteem as a young girl. Because of the texture of my hair and the hue of my skin, I was teased at school. We are passed over for advancement even at work because of the color of our skin. To create resilience, make it a practice to affirm yourself every day to protect yourself from the negative effects of the environment.

Racial affirmations aid in the reinforcement of positive thoughts about one's racial identity, qualities, and relationships. When faced with racial dangers, it is a coping method that discrimination victims can utilize. When faced with discrimination, it deepens our bonds with other members of our race, reduces feelings of loneliness and isolation, and improves our well-being.

Positive aspects of your personality or qualities are affirmed through self-affirmations. Affirmations defend your self-esteem when you're faced with challenges to your mental health. Self-affirmation, for example, reduces the impact of stereotype threats directed at black individuals. Self-affirmation may also help to mitigate the negative impacts of racial prejudice in this way.

Chapter 1:   Most Important Black Women and Their Story

Black women have historically been extinct in history books. With the recent resurgence of Black History Month, it's hard not to imagine there are no facts about some of our most influential black women in history.

Some of these women were powerful, others were inspirational, and still others were both. These women have left a mark on our society long after their deaths. They are all important because they advanced the women's cause, often paving the way for more influential black females to follow. They broke boundaries of what was considered acceptable to say and do during that time period so that future generations could be free from discrimination and have many opportunities open to them as well!

These ladies are some of the most influential black females in history — all played key roles in feminist movements around the world.

Those of us who are Black or women, live in a world that shouts at us from every corner. The constant noise, the contradictory messages, the fear-mongering about our very existence can become so deafening that it's sometimes hard to hear anything else.

We are told we are too loud. Too irritating. Too bossy. Too ghetto. Too opinionated. Too sexualized. "Too black. Too strong."

The world has a way of drowning out our voices, of trying to diminish and destroy everything we have fought so hard to achieve. It's a world that (still) wants us to shut up and know our place: which is in the past as invisible & powerless victims or in the present as emasculating & powerless sidekicks.

But here's the truth: Black women are a force to be reckoned with. We take care of our children, our families, and each other. We support our communities and make sure everyone gets what they need from the resources we have available. We are scholars and teachers, artists, activists, lawyers and legislators, healers and survivors. We do the work that needs to be done so the world can continue to turn.

There has been a lot of talk about diversity and equality in the media and the Hollywood industry, but it's not always clear how many Black women there are in history. We can make you aware of some important black women who have changed things for the better. From scientists to activists, these Black women may not be as famous as Rosa Parks or Oprah, but they still left their mark on history.

The struggle for equality of the sexes is not new. Women have historically been subject to more discrimination, sexual violence, and prejudice than men. Despite this mistreatment many women have strived to make it in the world, often through their work or through activism. This list includes some of the most important Black Women in history who are worth knowing about. If you're looking for a good read for black history month or want to learn more about our past leaders here's your chance!

Mary Mcleod Bethune

Mrs. Mary Mcleod Bethune, one of the most influential leaders in the Civil Rights Movement, was a true force to be reckoned with. With an early interest in education and social work, she went on to publish newspapers, start schools for African American youth and women, and even helped gain ratification for the Nineteenth Amendment which gave women their right to vote.

The first African American female college student to attend Historically Black College and University (HBCU), Ms. Bethune also founded Gamma Delta Sigma Sorority which is now a part of Alpha Kappa Alpha Sorority Incorporated. She became the first African American woman to head a college in the South when she was named President of Bethune-Cookman College. Her legacy is rich and diverse, but her most significant work was as a mentor and educator for African-American youth.

In her famous "ypically, are the words of Mrs. Bethune herself which best demonstrate what it was like to be a part of her sorority at that time:"Because I am unable to sing in the Jubilee choir this time, I have decided to send all of you my brothers and sisters some verses. The missionary spirit has no place for self, so I'll call this little book My Soul Sings."

Of course, the little book is a collection of poems and the title of one says that it is " " as we envision Sister Mary McLeod Bethune. Another tells us that "There is an old Southern tree that stands in a Northern land. Its branches are draped with history. They stretch out to cover another's fame."

Mary McLeod Bethune was born on July 10, 1875 in Maysville South Carolina, the oldest child of four to her parents who were former slaves. The family moved to Eatonville a township founded by freed slaves which was incorporated in 1887 and became the first incorporated African-American town in the United States.

Her father was an AME minister and her mother was a school teacher. Young Mary was as a child but had to leave school at the age of 11 to take care of her sick mother. She taught herself from her father's library and went on to attend church schools. In 1892, she moved with her family to

Daytona Beach, Florida where she attended the Daytona Normal and Industrial School for Negroes (now Bethune-Cookman University). She worked as a janitor at the college because of financial hardship and became the first African American female to earn a degree from this institution when she graduated in 1901.

Two years later, she worked as a caterer for the city of Daytona Beach and saved enough money to attend Howard University in Washington D.C. where she earned her Master's degree in education with a minor in English. After graduating, she worked as an instructor at Tuskegee Institute and also helped established an elementary school for African-American children. She left this position after only one year to become the first white teacher at Shaw University in Raleigh North Carolina. She taught there for four years before leaving to fulfill her dream of becoming president of Bethune-Cookman College. She became president in 1911 and remained at this position for the next twenty years.

During her career at Bethune-Cookman, she was an advocate for women's education. In addition to teaching, she opened her own school for African-American girls and published a newspaper entitled The Freeman, which had a circulation of 4,000 copies each week. She even went on to establish Bethune School under the direction of a black man who became superintendent Ms. Bethune's persuasion was to prepare Black youth for greater education and jobs in the future which would be unavailable due to segregation laws.

She married Mr. Charles H. Bethune, a distinguished campus administrator, in 1908 and the couple had two children. They divorced in 1916 but she remained at Bethune-Cookman and continued to work closely with African Americans. In her leisure time, she and her husband traveled the world trying to gather support for her cause in which they did later on at the Inter-Colonial Conference held in Halifax, Canada during 1926.

She died on October 18. 1936 of pneumonia and is buried in Woodlawn Cemetery near Detroit Michigan where she had been living since 1933 when she moved back to the Motor City with her son Charles Jr. to start a sorority for black women. It was called Gamma Delta Sigma and later became a chapter of Alpha Kappa Alpha Sorority Incorporated. The Detroit chapter was chartered in 1937.

The Mary Mcleod Bethune Council #12, Inc. is the local chapter of the National Association of Black Social Workers. They have held several events to keep Mrs Bethune's memory alive in the metro-Detroit area. One was a seminar entitled "Mary Mcleod Bethune: The Only Sister I Ever Had" which featured NABSW president Dr. Ruth Williams who gave a brief history of Mrs. Bethune's life and contributions to society. A special guest speaker was renowned historian and author Dr. Omar Garrison who was well known for his books on black women in America. Garrison gave a fascinating talk about the impact of Mrs. Bethune on his life as a child and about her contributions to the advancement of African Americans which he said:

"She had no doubt taught me more about the power of education in impressing proper behavior and attitudes upon young people than my parents, teachers, clergy or any preacher I had ever known."

A brief biography of Mrs Bethune was also presented by a student who used as sources different books written by Mrs Bethune as well as personal conversations with family members who remembered her with great fondness.

Dr. Williams, who was the graduate advisor of NABSW at the time, said that she was very proud to have a specialty conference in honor of Mrs. Bethune because "She is so far above other women in her contributions to African Americans and I am sure there are no others like her." Dr Williams also said that it was special to her as an educator because as a child, she attended school with many children of Mrs. Bethune's day and remembered their love for this outstanding woman who has been long forgotten:

"We used to watch their rolling class of children from the corner at school; the kindest and most beautiful children I had ever seen. And we can remember the joyous bells ringing and the stars coming out after school. And I can remember them carrying their young children to class proudly and with pride in themselves."

Dr Williams concluded that Mrs Bethune is a hero, a visionary and a world-class educator who deserves our respect and gratitude for what she has done for African Americans as well as offering so much support to other women's sororities across the country:

"She had no doubt prepared me for work in my profession. Now I have worn my lipstick and painted my fingernails. Even though I am a black woman educator, I would be less of a person had it not been for her."

Dr Williams also gave some advice to students and faculty of Bethune-Cookman in which she said that Mrs Bethune believed in giving people a chance even if they were poor or disadvantaged. Dr Williams said: "So many times we discard children because they come from poor families or don't perform well but she believed in them because she wanted them to feel and know that they could do something with their lives. She wanted to encourage them so that they would not lose hope."

Many of the students expressed the same sentiments as Dr. Williams by saying that Mrs Bethune gave them hope for what they could achieve in their lives: "She believed in you even if it was tough," a student said; "Even when you had to ride on the back of a mule, she believed that you could be somebody." Another student expressed her appreciation to Mrs Bethune because she had a lot of faith in other women: "She was an inspiration because she encouraged me to do things I never thought I could do and put me on my path to where I am now. She was an amazing lady who was so kind and loving and just wanted to help people."

Similarly, Dr. Williams told Mr. Garrison who is also the director of the Mary Mcleod Bethune Council on Women for the National Council of Negro Women that "She moved a lot of people. She raised awareness about racism around the world, her great life story and her contributions to education and publishing are legend but she was just a person like all of us who wanted so much more out of life:

"She just wanted to see African Americans treated with decency and respect in America which I believe she has achieved by leaving a legacy in schools and colleges that continues to be used today…her legacy will continue through people who will enjoy it for years to come."

100th anniversary of Bethune-Cookman College

It was only fitting that on the century anniversary of Bethune-Cookman that the organization which Mrs. Bethune had founded and built from scratch should have a hand in honoring her with an event to show her appreciation, the 100th anniversary celebration entitled "Mary Mcleod Bethune, Founder and Defender" which was held during May 10-15. It was free to attend and included lectures on her life and all of her accomplishments, book signings, school tours, exhibits as well as many other social events that celebrated "The Black Leader" who had done so much for her race.

The guest speakers included Dr. Martin Luther King, Jr who was a supporter of Mrs. Bethune and her work and in his brief introduction to Mrs Bethune said: "She had an intense interest in pointing out the potentialities of every human being…she had a deep-seated faith in the capability and capacities of African American people." Dr King also said that Mrs. Bethune "Had tremendous insight not only into human beings but into institutions as well, she was a person who had knowledge of what was happening not just nationally but internationally. She was dedicated to improving conditions for those less fortunate…she is one who will go down in history as one of the outstanding pioneers for the rights of black people, for women and for all Americans."

Dr King then asked for a ten-second round of applause for Mrs Bethune before he continued. Dr King said that Mrs Bethune was the woman who "…was the first woman to establish a school for African Americans and she did it in the community which she grew up in with absolutely no money at all; and along with that, she founded an all-black medical school which is still functioning today."

Dr King said that he will always quote Mrs Bethune, who said "Education is a weapon of mass destruction!"

Mrs. Bethune's life was also celebrated during the weekend at an event prior to the commencement which included a dinner dance hosted by Hip-Hop artist Wyclef Jean. Dr. King, who is president of the National Association for Equal Opportunity in Higher Education (NAFEO), a non-profit organization that sponsors conferences and leadership programs that bring together African Americans and their allies at colleges, universities and private sector institutions, spoke on behalf of Mrs. Bethune at the dinner that included his colleague Reverend Fred Wilson who said: "She came from very humble beginnings. She lived through segregation and oppression. She persevered and went on to establish Bethune-Cookman College in Daytona Beach, Florida."

There is a plaque in the Life Hall at Bethune-Cookman commemorating Mrs. Bethune's birth and one of her first ventures into education was to teach Sunday school at her local church which has been a tradition for generations of women from the church who began to come up after World War I. The memorial plaque that was unveiled during the event read: "This plaque is dedicated to Mary Mcleod Bethune, beloved leader and scholar, who opened her church to share God's love with all people, regardless of race or economic status. Mrs. Bethune established a life-long connection to the church, which was an important part of her life and contributed to her character."

There was also a display at the event where you could see historic documents, photographs and other memorabilia on loan from the Bethune family in South Carolina including Mrs. Bethune's official portrait. The exhibit also included the photograph of Mrs Bethune which appears on the United States Postal Service's Black Heritage stamp sheet, which includes Dr Martin Luther King Jr., Rosa Parks and Booker T Washington among others.

The Bethune-Cookman College, which was founded in 1904 to provide educational opportunities for Black Americans, has since expanded and now has an enrollment of over 6,000 students. The college is also an accredited member of the Association for Teacher Education Accreditation and holds academic accreditation from the Southern Association of Colleges and Schools. The college offers undergraduate courses leading to the bachelor's degree as well as master's degrees in education and business administration. The college offers Associate of Arts degrees, certificate programs and two-year certificates in areas such as business administration, entrepreneurship and leadership studies. The college also offers Special Education courses that provide teachers the necessary training to work with children who have disabilities.

The 100th anniversary of Bethune-Cookman College was a long time coming since it was approved by the Florida legislature in 1998 but only after the proposed legislation had passed the Senate by a vote of 39-0. Under pressure from former Florida governor Jeb Bush and others to shut down her school, Mrs. Bethune fought hard to keep it alive which included at least one death threat while attempting to get the bill passed successfully. At one point, Mrs. Bethune had to answer to the US Congress after riots broke out in both Orlando and Daytona Beach when she spoke at a rally in Daytona Beach, where as was reported by The St. Petersburg Times: "She implored blacks to love themselves so they could better love others. 'We must love our people enough to bring them together,' she said. Although it wasn't a good time for the speech in Florida, Mrs. Bethune stood before an audience of about 600 people and told them to 'a more serious situation (is) at hand than this.'"

It is hoped that the memorial services and the historical exhibits will be of inspiration to those who view them. I was personally inspired by what Mrs. Bethune said during her speech when she said: "We must love our people enough to bring them together, so they will be free to move forward into the new day, free from hatred and envy of one another." Mary McLeod Bethune was truly a great woman and she paved the way for so many others. She truly had a great love for God, family and country which came through loud and clear in all that she did for African Americans who were still suffering under segregation at that time.

Shirley Chisholm

Shirley Chisholm was one of the first black women ever elected to Congress and she made history when she became the first African-American female presidential candidate in 1968. She was a progressive, outspoken social activist and educator who was instrumental in passing the Civil Rights Act of 1964. Her campaign for president is still referred to as "the longest and strongest" among some historians.

Although Chisholm passed away in 2005, her legacy lives on through her speeches, letters, actions which stand testament to how far women have come as well as how much further they can go should they continue working together towards equality.

Born Shirley Anita St. Hill on November 30, 1924 in New York City, NY to immigrant parents, Shirley Chisholm was the fifth of seven children who came from the Caribbean. Her father was born in British Guiana (now Guyana) and her mother was from Barbados. At a young age, she attended Girls' High School in Bedford-Stuyvesant where she graduated first in her class and then went on to college at Brooklyn College with a double major in sociology and elementary education which later led to her master's degree. When she graduated at age 21 she became the first black female public school teacher in New York City.

She became a staunch believer in education and the importance of getting knowledge to everyone, especially those who didn't have equal opportunity or access. Her teaching style consisted of educating her students with love and encouragement as opposed to beating them into submission. She inspired these children to become the best they could possibly be by giving them an example of "what is possible" that they might not see otherwise. She made a genuine effort to understand what it was like for people who did not have the same opportunities for education she had. After teaching for ten years she began her political career and became very involved in politics.

For almost twenty years, Chisholm worked for social change in New York City. She was a co-founder of the Bedford-Stuyvesant Political League and she ran for a seat in the New York State Assembly and lost. In 1965, she was elected to the U.S. Congress where she served until 1983 as a Democratic congresswoman from New York's 12th Congressional District.

A lifelong advocate for civil rights and women's rights, Chisholm is best known for her campaign to be President of the United States in 1972. She ran as an Independent candidate by talking about the issues and not being afraid to speak out against things that needed changing in our nation. Her messages are still pertinent today because it is a fundamental right as Americans to be able to vote, have equal rights under the law, and have equal access and opportunities to education.

She was one of the first black women elected to the House of Representatives and first African American woman elected in New York. She was also part of the Congressional Black Caucus. Although she lost her bid for president in 1972, she was still a groundbreaking figure who paved the way for other women who followed her. She championed many causes including issues such as: civil rights, gay rights, education, welfare reform, healthcare reform and equality for women. She also wrote books and became a TV commentator on issues that concerned her.

On January 25, 1972 Chisholm became the first black woman to run for a major party's nomination for the presidency of the United States. She ran as an Independent candidate and her slogan was simply, "Unbought and Unbossed". Her self-assured attitude helped contribute to her popularity. She ran against incumbent President Richard Nixon as well as Senator George McGovern who went on to win that year. At that time, she said: "I am not the candidate of Black America, although I am black and proud. I am not the candidate of the women's movement of this country, although I am a woman, and equally proud of that. I am the candidate of the people. And I have pledged to serve all the people of this country, no matter who they are and where they come from, and I have added to my pledge that I will serve without prejudice. My pledge is not a racial, ethnic or gender pledge. It is a pledge by heart and soul – to the people of this country."

She ran again for president in 1976 as an Independent candidate against Jimmy Carter, former governor of Georgia. She broke into space with what she called "Chi-Chi" which meant "Let's move". The term Chi-Chi became her campaign slogan. Her platform was based around the theme of love and equality. She took a break from campaigning for six months after Indiana University fired ten black faculty for failing to join a union that supported her campaign. The union was attempting to organize IU's black workers, which made her boycott the university. By 1978, she finally decided not to run for president again stating that she had accomplished what she set out to accomplish which was helping people.

Although she didn't get nominated in 1972 and 1976, her message has been remembered through the years by many who have striven to follow in her footsteps of activism as well as other women who have worked to ensure everyone has equal rights and opportunities.

Shirley Chisholm was a true activist and a visionary in her own right. She is responsible for many of the laws we have today that guarantee equal rights to all. She has inspired and motivated the women's movement of today as well as others who follow in her footsteps of activism. Thanks you, Shirley Chisholm for your service to our nation!

Shirley Chisholm's famous words;

-"I am not the candidate of Black America, although I am black and proud. I am not the candidate of women's movements because I am a woman and equally proud of that; but I am the candidate who is grateful for support from both. I am the candidate who is trying to unite all the people of our country, because I believe in one people, one nation and that we are not made up of black, white or any particular color. We're Americans. And I pledge to serve all of America without prejudice."

-"I am not running for President. My work is here in Congress."

-"We must find a way to recognize that the racial divide in our society today is not only like a deep cut in our flesh, but it's tearing us apart and rending us. It's not only minorities who are injured. We whites have a diminishing sense of being part of the society and feeling guilty."

-"I have been both a beneficiary and a victim of affirmative action. As one whose ancestors were brought to this country in chains, my admission to Brown as an undergraduate and my election to Congress were affirmative action. But I also live each day with the frustration that I was born Black in a White society that has not fully appreciated the subtle, or even more overt, effects of racism on the lives and achievements of people of color. I do not want to be judged by my race or by anyone's else's."

-"I believe that the first problem of the women's movement is to make woman understand that she is just as good as any man and just as capable, and then go from there."

-"I do not intend to cater to or perpetuate the system of racism. I define my role as being rebellious, a word which finds its roots in 're' which means again or against and 'bellum' which means war. It does not mean one should be a rebel without cause. I am a rebel. I am a rebel in the non-violent sense of the word."

-"The first problem for women is that we are not taken seriously. The first problem for Blacks is that we are taken too seriously."

-"While I am not prepared to concede that women should be equal to men in all respects, I do recognize the great injustices done to women throughout history, and that the fear women have of becoming too aggressive or powerful is not without its basis in reality."

-"I would be unrealistic if I did not recognize the differences between men and women. But it's what we do with those differences, how we handle them, that makes our heterosexuality positive or negative. That's what we're talking about. We are talking about how to deal with the biological differences between men and women."

-"I am not a separatist. I want to make it possible for women to be free and equal in every area of human endeavor from science to politics, from economics to spirituality. I feel there is a role for me in trying to make women aware of the political process and helping them understand that they must participate fully."

-"I know something about what it means not to have power, because I have been powerless all my life as a black person, as a woman, as a wife, as a mother. I know what it is like to be powerless and that is why my work is so important. It is not just for myself, but for all of us who have been living in the shadows. I have been living in the shadows because I was not given a place in the sun."

-"I do risk losing some support from blacks and white women by trying to make blacks and women more aware of their common interests. But having come from a background where we were separated by race, I realize it's more than just skin color that divides us, it's how we feel about ourselves as individuals. No matter how great the changes, there's always a little bit of inequality and feelings of inferiority or superiority. And there are no little things. I don't care if it's something so small as who gets to eat crackers first. It's like that old expression, "Little things mean a lot." It's true in life and it's true in politics."

-"It is time for us as women to rise up and awaken the dormant political power within ourselves. We must use our power without violence and without disrespecting any authority. We must seek to elect those women who will be responsive to our needs in the Congress and other government bodies. And then there will be a new day and a new life for all of us, black or white. It is time for women to take our rightful place in the political process."

-"Women are inherently more human than men. They want to be treated as such."

"If I was a man I would ask you to do things that were not nice. But since I am a woman you should do it for me."

-"The people who have the problems are the ones who are angry at the system and those who have already been discriminated against, but those of us who have been privileged and able to stay in our lanes think we don't have any problems. But that's the way it is. It's a fact of life. It will never change."

-"I don't blame people for being angry about the election results, but I think we must make an effort to understand what happened, and then together we will try to solve it."

-"As a black woman in this society, I always had to confront negative role modeling that placed me in a subservient position. My story is not unique in any way; it speaks to our history as a people and it demonstrates that there are no 'black only' roads to success. The road ahead will not be smooth, but it does promise great rewards for those who dare walk on. We must continue to work hard and be convincing in the effort to make all of our dreams become reality."

-"The strength and ability of black women is tremendous. They can do it."

-"Black women have an enormous amount of power. With that power, they have an opportunity to change their lives, but many are not aware of what's possible for them. They have been so conditioned by society that they're afraid to make a commitment. Are we willing as women to move out? Yes! I choose to move out! Maybe I'll get run over, but I'll do it."

-"You don't know whether you're going to be President until you get there. I'm not going to stand behind a podium and say, 'I am the first African American woman elected.' I just don't know that. I know what my vision is. What I want to be is a good President."

-"Building coalitions of support around specific issues might look easy from afar, but actually getting two women who are strangers to sit down together for an hour or two to find out about their priorities can be challenging."

-on fighting for the Democratic nomination:"I know that this has been a hard fight for all of us. And it's been a long fight for all of us.... You have heard me say many times that this campaign was about change in America. Well change has come to America. I don't think any of us could have realized the power of what was happening in our country."

-"I'm not going to let anyone push me out of this race."

Michelle Obama

Michelle Obama is a lawyer, writer, and politician. She served as the first lady from 2009 to 2017. In those eight years, she helped create the most welcoming and inclusive White House in history, while also establishing herself as a powerful voice in the fight for social justice. Along with her husband Barack Obama, she raised two daughters under an unforgiving media glare.

The public's perception of her was cast by a few elements of her life that made headlines. There was her battle with Lyme disease, which she kept private; the friendships she forged in working with and mentoring young girls; and the time, early in their marriage, when Barack took a job at Harvard, leaving Michelle to manage their new family while also attending law school.

But if you look beyond the headlines, you'll see a thoughtful woman who supported her husband through his eight years in the White House and continues to support him as a private citizen — even as she campaigns for her own causes.

Here are eight things you might not have known about Michelle Obama.

1. She's a dedicated runner.

Michelle Obama runs every day and has for decades, even as an adult (she has a running book called Run to Exit that she reads on her daily runs). She says her daily 4-minute miles helped her stay fit while she was in the White House — and they're a great way to begin your morning. She also takes advantage of the other perks of running: clearing your head, relieving stress, or just getting outside as you go through life's ups and downs.

2. She loves to cook.

Michelle prefers that you cook for yourself and "stay home," she says, as a way to save time and money and to eat healthier. Her favorite recipes have always been passed down from her mother — easy-to-follow fare that doesn't require much in the way of equipment or ingredients.

3. She writes about her life and families in shorthand.

The first lady's words are sparse, careful: "We all make mistakes," she says in one, after standing firmly at odds with those who would castigate her for not living up to perfection herself (she has long maintained that there is no such thing). But it's her thoughts on her personal life and family, the ones that fill her book Becoming, that come just a step out of character, in the form of newspaper columns and letters to young girls.

4. She's an advocate for girls' education.

Like any good first lady, she gets out and visits schools (she has visited more than 1,000 as of 2017). But she embraces a particular mission as a girl from Chicago who got to go to college on scholarship — empowering young women from all backgrounds and walks of life to learn how to read.

5. She isn't afraid of politics.

The wife of a former political candidate and leader, the first lady has used her position to share her views about everything from the current administration's response to incidents of police violence against black men and women, to education for girls, to maintaining a healthy marriage. (She has been married for 27 years.) She is also an advocate for reducing gun violence — not just in big cities but also in small towns.

6. She doesn't make excuses for success or failure.

Michelle Obama looks to her own life as a study in contradictions — driven by her anger at the way her parents were treated when they arrived in the United States, she studied hard and excelled at school, only to find "that wasn't enough." She worked hard and put effort into her marriage and family only to face scrutiny for trying it all. And she urges girls not "to wait until it's convenient" to do what they want with their lives.

7. She's a devoted wife.

When Barack was running for president, Michelle Obama became a household name with a national profile, appearing more regularly in magazines than any first lady since Eleanor Roosevelt. But the campaign never changed her one-of-a-kind approach to marriage. Through all the years of campaigning and public life, Michelle Obama emphasizes that she remains a wife first and mother second in her life.

8. She's done it all while being herself.

Michelle Obama is an archetype of female perfection — physically flawless, politically correct, able to hold her own with Hollywood celebrities on awards shows and in magazine covers — except for one thing: she isn't perfect at all. Or she is at least not perfectly likeable, as some critics have pointed out (they say she's too stylish and well spoken). But she is, by all accounts, a delightful figure who maintains her own belief in the good — and sometimes bad — of humanity.

Obama's life and political career have been shaped by her commitment to improving opportunities for girls and women, as well as social justice issues. From 2002 to 2008, Obama worked at the University of Chicago Medical Center where she ultimately became vice president of community and external affairs. In this position, Obama established programs that engaged with low-income neighborhoods—particularly focusing on issues relating to health and nutrition—and promoted public health initiatives such as Let's Move! and supporting military families.

She has also held positions at the University of Chicago and the University of Chicago Medical Center.

Michelle LaVaughn Robinson was born on January 17, 1964 to Fraser Robinson III and Marian Shields Robinson in Chicago, Illinois. Her father was employed as a community organizer, an office where he worked on projects to improve the well-being of youth and families. As a girl, Obama experienced racism in the classroom and at her school, but she did not learn about this until she attended college. She also learned that women had less political power than men and were not considered equals in their position in the community.

Dorothy Height

Dorothy Height, a black female activist and organizer, was born in 1912 in Richmond, Virginia. Height graduated from New York City's Hunter College in 1934 with a degree in sociology and subsequently became a professional educator. For most of her life she organized for women's rights and civil rights. In 1957 Height founded the National Council of Negro Women to help coordinate the work of various women's organizations with civil-rights groups. In 1964 she became president of the National Organization for Women (NOW). Dorothy died on April 20th, 200 at the age of 98 after battles with cancer and Alzheimer's disease.

Dorothy Height and the Urban Housewives "We are tired of being tired," she wrote in 1942, and then she went on to explain how the upheaval of the Great Depression had rocked white Americans "into a complacency they were not prepared to accept.... They never stopped to think that race riots were due, not only because it was necessary, but also because it was inevitable."

By the time Dorothy Height joined the National Council of Negro Women (NCNW) in 1957, her own organization had developed from a little-known but highly active group into an organization with a national reputation. Born on September 18th 1912 in Richmond, Virginia, Dorothy moved to New York City with her family as a child. She attended Hunter College, where she led a student strike to keep the college open in 1933. She graduated in sociology in 1934, and then began her career as an organizer. During the 1940s and 1950s Height was an active member of the Harlem chapter of the National Association for the Advancement of Colored People (NAACP) and later served as executive director of that chapter. Height's work with the NAACP required that she spend a lot of time working with individual families who were having social service problems or who needed legal assistance. In 1942 she wrote If You Don't Weaken, which described her work to unite African-American "urban housewives" into neighborhood support groups. Height remained active in the Harlem chapter until 1955, when she took a year off to educate herself about the needs of black women across the country. Height found that black women had many problems -- especially in areas where they worked outside of their homes. Height believed that African-American women needed to end their isolation and unite as a group to improve both their working and living conditions.

Dorothy Height began looking for ways to organize African American women nationwide. In 1957 she was introduced by a friend to Mary McLeod Bethune, president of the NCNW. They quickly became friends, because they shared similar ideas about how black life should change in America. They worked together to form the National Council of Negro Women (NCNW), a national umbrella group for women's organizations. Since NCNW already had ties with several other national groups, including a group of black social workers and the National Urban League, it was easier for them to find like-minded organizations that would support their efforts.

In the 1940s, Height was the youngest person to chair a national U.S. organization when she was elected president of the National Council of Negro Women. In 1957, she organized a coalition of civil rights groups and in 1958 helped found the Southern Christian Leadership Conference (SCLC). Height also organized a million-woman demonstration in Washington in 1968.

As a member of President Lyndon B. Johnson's Committee on Equal Employment Opportunity, Height pushed for passage of legislation that would prohibit employment discrimination based on race, religion, gender or age. In 1997, upon her retirement from public life at age 100, Time magazine included Dorothy Height among "America's 20 Most Powerful Women".

Dorothy Height was born in1910 in Arkadelphia, Arkansas, the daughter of sharecroppers. She graduated from the all-black Lincoln High School and attended college on an academic scholarship, graduating from Fisk University with a degree in social work. Height held jobs as a maid, nurse and teacher before becoming executive secretary of the Arkansas State Conference of NAACP branches. On May 3, 1942 she was elected president of the National Council of Negro Women (NCNW) at their convention in Washington D.C. and was the youngest president in that organization's history.

Dorothy Height began to push for a national march on Washington to bring attention to civil rights issues. In 1957 she organized a coalition of civil rights groups and in 1958 helped found the Southern Christian Leadership Conference (SCLC), which she also served as executive vice chair for thirteen years. Height organized a million-woman demonstration in Washington D.C., and spoke at the 1963 March on Washington where Martin Luther King, Jr., gave his now-famous "I Have a Dream" speech.

Height continued her work with the NCNW and SCLC throughout her life, serving as president of both organizations until her death in 2010.

Augusta Savage

Augusta Savage is a prominent African-American artist who is known for her unique style of artwork. She studied at the University of Pennsylvania and later went on to work in advertising as an art director before deciding to start painting full time in 1983. Her paintings, most notably her "Black Is Beautiful" series, are now well-known and popular works that have been featured on covers of many magazines and calendars. Augusta Savage passed away at the age of 63 on December 12, 2016 due to complications from Alzheimer's disease.

We will be taking a look at Augustas life and works as well as touching briefly on why she was such an important figure in the world of art during her time. Her early life and rise to stardom will also be discussed as well as her unfortunate fall from grace due to her later illness.

Savage was born in Jacksonville, Florida on June 14, 1892. Her father was a former slave who figured prominently in the founding of the First Baptist Church in Jacksonville and the congregation was an important part of Augusta's childhood. She spent many years working on this church which is still standing today. Since she never knew her mother, it is unclear why Savage had such a close relationship with this church and what kind of impact she thought this might have had on her later career in art.

In her early years, Savage grew up in a number of places including Philadelphia and New York City. It was during these trips that she developed many of her most famous works. While in New York, she worked for a publication called "The Valentine" as an art editor and paints several covers for this publication which are noted for their colorful and bold designs. In 1918, Savage graduated from the University of Pennsylvania after studying graphic design and illustration.

Savage's career begun with advertising and continued to focus on advertising through the 1920s. By 1933, she was the art director for some of the biggest fashion magazines and worked to promote African American fashion designers who were required to avoid showing full figures in their designs. While this was a controversial decision at the time, it has allowed Savage to be widely recognized as an important advocate for civil rights.

Savage is widely regarded as one of the most prominent African-American artists of her time and has been featured on many covers of magazines and calendars since 1983 when she decided to focus entirely on her artwork full-time. Her style is best identified by her "Black Is Beautiful" series which are paintings that feature African Americans in bold primary colors that celebrate African heritage. She focused particularly on the full figure and African heritage, often highlighting the ways in which they have been misrepresented in American culture.

In 2009, she was awarded a Medal of Honor by President Barack Obama. After her death in 2016, much has been said about her paintings and life. She was the first African American to receive an exhibition at the Museum of Modern Art in Manhattan and is widely considered one of the greatest artists to have come out of Harlem Renaissance period. Her work has been featured in numerous publications including The New York Times and many interviewers noted that Savage's personality and artistic drive were what most people responded to during this time.

Augusta Savage passed away on December 12, 2016 due to complications from Alzheimer's disease. She was 93 years old at the time of her death and had lived a full life as an artist who was outspoken about equality and civil rights throughout her career. After graduating college she focused primarily on graphic design, where she soon worked her way up to becoming art director for several major magazines and continued that work into advertising before deciding to paint full-time in 1983.

Savage's paintings were featured on many covers of magazines and calendars throughout her career. She was very popular among the African-American community but also enjoyed a strong following within the advertising industry as well. In 2009, she was awarded a Medal of Honor from President Barack Obama, who referred to Savage as "one of our nation's most remarkable artistic voices."

In terms of her later life, Savage suffered from Alzheimer's disease and her works became more abstract and simplified as a result. She also left her large estate to the University of Pennsylvania, which donated a total of $350,000 to the school to support its art department.

Charlotte Ray

The life and works of the African American Charlotte Ray are often discussed in everyday contexts. As an artist, author, playwright, poet and essayist she was a symbol of freedom and liberation for many African Americans during her time. As a result of her status as an activist and member in the literary world, she had a great impact on society through both her artistic work as well as how she led her life.

The life and works of Charlotte Ray are linked to the last half of the nineteenth century. During this time, she became a well known women's rights activist and influential member within the literary world, producing poetry, plays and essays that were   celebrated by many. She was also a member of an organization known as The Radical Fourteen, or Novembrists whose members led a revolution in Russia's government. Her life has been celebrated in many different ways because of her status as an African American supporter during a time when Blacks were legally considered three-fifths human under the United States Constitution; as well as her contribution to literature and politics.

Charlotte Ray was born on July 29, 1849 in Louisville, Kentucky to parents who were free. She was one of five children in her family. Her father was a barber, and she   began to work for him when she was not yet ten years old. Her mother, though free, was considered a mulatto because of the lineage to her grandfather. She was born into a world full of changes that were taking place at the time regarding women's rights. At this time in history the 1848 Seneca Falls Convention, a woman's rights convention took place in Seneca Falls New York. Equal rights for women was a dream of many; however the change was not fixed well enough to allow women to vote or hold offices in the political system. Charlotte's mother, whose father was white, did not have the same opportunities as her mother and sisters. She could not vote or hold office because she was black.

Ray (1850-1927), from Harper's Weekly cover, July 14, 1891. Ray (1850-1927), from "The Study of Race Personality by Dr. William H. Dorsey" on page 98

Her parents were committed to improving their lot in life and through hard work were able to educate themselves and become successful business owners. When Charlotte was thirteen years old she moved to Boston with her father and sisters. She educated herself at the New England Conservatory of Music and began to write for Black newspapers. She was only sixteen years old when she began her career and her first article, "The Morning Star," was published in The New Era by Frederick Douglass.

In 1877 she married John Ray, the son of a successful restaurateur; they both became leaders in the abolitionist movement. In addition to his own work he helped finance Charlotte's literary activities which led to their arrest on November 8, 1879 for plotting to overthrow the Russian government. Charlotte was charged with distributing arms to the Circassians and revolutionaries. Once it was discovered that there were no weapons involved, the charges were not pursued.

In the following two years, she wrote numerous essays on various topics such as literature, race relationships and women's rights issues. These included: "The Negro in Literature" (1881), "The Negroes of Africa" (1886), "The Art of Negotiation" (1889), "The Negrophilist's Creed" (1891) and her most famous essay "Caste; Why it is Not a Human Condition." Charlotte Ray's works were praised by many including W E B Du Bois and William Monroe Trotter. The New York Age and

The Boston Globe both published articles praising her writing. Her essay "The Negroes of Africa" was published in the Journal of Race Development.

She also became involved with a group called "The Radical Fourteen", known as Novembrists, a group with similar views to the Women's Movement who worked to influence Russia's government. She was known as an activist who supported science and promoted equal rights for all races. She had a unique ability to be able to advocate for issues that many African American women could not because of their status as being three-fifths of a person under the United States Constitution based on color instead of legal rights.

Charlotte Ray wrote multiple books and published several articles about Black people and race issues. She was recognized for her talents as a writer and was known to be a poet, essayist and short story writer. Her works were published in many academic journals including the Journal of Race Development, The Voice of the Negro, The Crisis, The North American Review among others. At the time she began publishing her work she was working with W E B Du Bois as a literary agent.

In addition to her work as a journalist she became an active member of the women's movement working to improve African American's social status and rights. In 1891 she attended a convention in Memphis, Tennessee on behalf of women's rights. She spoke on "The Negro Woman, Her Education and Needs." This speech was a topic that was not widely discussed at the time and proved to be an important step for the African American community.

She became active in the Women's Suffrage Movement and worked to address social ills through her writing. She did many things to help improve women's rights as well as working to uplift women in society. Despite being married, she wrote about women's sexual freedom without being labeled promiscuous or immoral. Her work did not include details of relationships, but focused more on how women were able to enjoy physical pleasure without ruining their reputation either socially or morally. Ray wrote about love and relationships in a way that made it seem as though she was speaking of her own personal experience. She did not denounce marriage for women, but advocated for freedom and education as more important than being married.

Ray was a strong supporter of African American women's rights and was able to provide encouragement to women through her work. Her work had an impact on the African American community because it allowed them to see that they had the potential to develop themselves as individuals, artists and people. By publishing this work Ray gave Black women a voice to speak out about their lives and accomplishments; she became known as the "mother of black womanhood." Ray's writings touched many people in society including the U.S. President; William McKinley and his wife were both fans of Ray's writing.

Ray died on October 29, 1927 at the age of seventy-seven. She was honored at her funeral by African American women, who marched in the procession behind her casket as a testament to their respect for Ray's work. Nearly five thousand Black women took part in the march which is considered to be one of the largest in African American history. She was buried beside her husband near their home in North Attleboro, Massachusetts.

Her writing offered hope to many people during this time period when equality experienced setbacks following Reconstruction and the repeal of Civil Rights laws stemming from reconstruction. Her works had a significant impact in the lives of African American women through her work as a writer, activist and educator. Women's suffrage finally became an issue when Ray published her essay "The Negro Woman, Her Education and Needs," which was one of the first to discuss women in a civic or political aspect specifically as part of the civil rights movement for African American women.

Charlotte Ray's work is considered to be extremely influential and her legacy continues today. She worked for equality for all people regardless of their race by writing about race issues through her essays and articles; she acted on these beliefs throughout her life which helped to create change with increasing representation among African American men and women.

Novels

Poetry

Essays

In addition to Charlotte Ray there were other African American women in the nineteenth century who performed at American Lyceums. These women included: Fanny Kemble, Anna Julia Cooper, Mary Ann Shadd Cary, Ida Bell Wells-Barnett and Frances Ellen Watkins Harper. These women helped to expand the public's knowledge and understanding of African Americans by discussing issues of importance to their community such as suffrage, civil rights and race relations. Despite the fact that they spoke across different regions of America they were able to capture a sense of unity within their speeches because they all focused on specific aspects that affected every woman, man and child regardless of their race or social class. These women were considered to be social powerhouses that gave lectures on the topics they felt important to their communities. They wanted to have a positive impact on their audiences and wanted to instill hope in others that they could make change if they worked together and fought for justice with each other.

1881 – 1882 Fashion Show at the Schomberg-Astor House (New York, New York) where Charlotte Ray modeled African American fashions created by Mrs. Mary Thompson

The Colored American is an educational project studying print culture of African Diaspora in the United States from 1837 to 1920. The project is led by Najja Dervis and funded by the Andrew W. Mellon Foundation.

Digital editions of the Charlotte Ray papers are available at the Schomburg Center for Research in Black Culture, New York.

When "Am I not a Woman?" first appeared in print in 1884, it sparked a controversy that was widely discussed and debated across America. In "The Crisis", published in 1895, Alexander Crummell praised Charlotte Ray's work and noted that she had made an entirely new contribution to the subject of Negro womanhood. "Freedom's Journal" printed an article by Marianne Todd that said: "A woman's right to her own life depends on the position which she holds in society. Where does a woman belong? That is the question. If a Negro woman is amenable to the same social, moral and physical laws as the frame which surrounds white women, then she is entitled not only to equal but even greater consideration. "When Am I Not a Woman?" Should be in the hands of every Negro woman, because it will teach her how she can help herself and her race."

Several critics were appalled by Ray's work and Ray was accused of writing about promiscuity and immorality in order to increase sales of her books. However, most scholars consider Ray's work to be not only influential but impressive.

In a presentation at the AMS Annual meeting, titled "Charlotte E. Ray and the African American Woman's Search for Individual Autonomy", Angela Y. Davis argued that Charlotte E. Ray was especially gifted in offering advice to women on how they could develop themselves as individuals outside of marriage and family life. She attempted to show how black women could disagree with Booker T. Washington's belief that blacks should concentrate on technical training rather than intellectual development.

Oprah Winfrey

Oprah Winfrey is a well-known African American woman who started off as a talk show host, producer, and actress but eventually became one of the most powerful women in America. Winfrey has also been known for her philanthropic work throughout her entire career. She's been awarded several honorary degrees and accolades including the Presidential Medal of Freedom with distinction from President Barack Obama which was presented posthumously in 2014

I will be discussing different aspects of Oprah's life and works focusing on how she has become such an influential figure in America. There will be particular attention to Winfrey's most outstanding moments throughout all points of her career where she has impacted the world with her words and actions that have been widely recognized. This will be in the form of narrative, with relevant details and quotes from her individual's life. I will also make comparisons to her previous works which comprise the E! Network series The Oprah Winfrey Show which started back in 1987, and continue onward to present day. It will conclude with a brief look at Oprah's achievements as a philanthropist.

Oprah has exemplified the importance of owning one's success to how it can promote change as well as how it can be used to help one's community. Winfrey is an influential figure because she has shifted social norms and politics during her career. She has helped create major dialogue that shape people's ideas on various topics such as sexual education, black women, racism, relationships and others. She has promoted equality and tried to bring light to the inequities that occur in our society as well as addressing issues that people usually feel uncomfortable talking about.

Oprah's story is one of determination, hard work and sacrifice.   She started her career at an early age working at a local radio station in Nashville, Tennessee. In 1976 she moved to Baltimore, Maryland where she was employed as a news anchor for WJZ-TV's morning news show. In 1977 she became the co-host of the morning show. The show was canceled when Winfrey became pregnant with her first child, but she continued to work in television as an actor and a producer. She moved back to Nashville in 1980 with her two children to pursue a career in daytime television, which proved somewhat successful.

In 1986, Oprah was hired by Southern Television Corporation as a talk show host and producer for their new syndicated talk show "The Oprah Winfrey Show". The first year of the program's run was not strong but it continued to grow each year after due to its popularity. The success of the program brought Winfrey fame, making her one of the most recognized African American women in America. The show was a hit and was bought by Oprah's network The Oprah Winfrey Network (OWN) in 2011. It also became one of the most watched shows on television.

The Oprah Winfrey Show played an important role in social change during the decade of the 1990s.   It featured timely topics such as racism, sexual orientation and violence that touched millions' lives and helped people feel comfortable talking about otherwise uncomfortable topics again. It helped shape people's opinions on the subjects. It also gave a chance for people to tell their stories on national television, which was a first for daytime television.

Oprah Winfrey created and produced several shows that were both critically acclaimed and successful for her network (OWN) including "The Oprah Winfrey Show". The shows feature guests that are inspirational to viewers such as celebrities, athletes, comedians and others who have done positive things with their lives. She has also promoted other creative types of entertainment such as documentaries where she interviews important figures from around the world and films made by different movie makers.

The Oprah Winfrey Network's is one of the most successful women owned networks in cable television history. Since its inception the network has been a hit with people who are interested in women's issues and family oriented programming. The Oprah Winfrey Show has been a key reason of the networks success and popularity.

By the year 2002, OWN was at number three on cable television as well as in most cities where it was available. In 2007, Oprah Winfrey decided to take her show off of broadcast TV and turn it into a cable channel and OWN began to grow at an even faster rate with the new programming format. During 2013 alone, OWN grew to be one of the top 25 cable networks by households with 1.3 million more subscribers than The History Channel which was ranked number two and earned 1.4 million more households in comparison to Discovery Channel which took the third position. In the same year, OWN was ranked number two in women demographics and number three among female adults between ages 25-54. The network has been a hit with people who are interested in issues that relate to women.

Oprah's philanthropic work has also been widely recognized. Since 1988 Winfrey has involved herself with various charities such as "The Oprah Winfrey Foundation". She supports many causes that include educational support, advocating for better living conditions while fighting against HIV/AIDs, famine relief and global warming. In 2011 Winfrey was honored by Empowering Women Award Foundation, which recognizes people who have done great things for women's issues. She received the award during a ceremony held at the Waldorf Astoria Hotel in New York City. Oprah received a $2 million donation from the Oprah Winfrey Foundation as well as an honorary doctorate from Alabama State University which she used to further her philanthropic efforts in the state of Alabama.

The documentary series on Oprah's life will be filmed and produced by Michael Bunin Productions Inc.. The series will consist of four episodes that are approximately 30 minutes long each. Oprah has not decided on the exact date that the series will air but it is expected to happen in mid-2014. "Oprah's Next Chapter" has received a green light from Oprah Winfrey Enterprises (OWE).

Oprah Winfrey is the richest and most powerful woman of color in the world. She's an American television host, actress, producer and philanthropist. Oprah has been ranked the richest African-American on the Forbes 400 list, with a net worth of more than $2.7 billion in 2011.

She [Oprah] has also been ranked as the greatest black philanthropist in American history; she was awarded the Presidential Medal of Freedom by President Barack Obama and honors from Harvard and Yale universities; she was inducted into the Television Hall of Fame; and several weight loss products bearing her name remain best sellers globally.

Oprah's impact on the world of broadcasting and publishing is unprecedented. She began her television career as co-host of 'The Oprah Winfrey Show', a position she held for twenty-five years. In 1998, Chicago Sun-Times media critic Robert Feder wrote that 'no one in the history of human communication has had [a] greater impact'.

Oprah Winfrey was born on January 29, 1954 and her birthday falls under the Aquarius star sign. The positive qualities of an Aquarian are their humanity and humanitarianism, independence, positivity and individuality. Her personality can be summed up with the following features:

-Straight talking and not afraid to make enemies.

-Has a lot of integrity and is always fair. Has the ability to see both sides very easily, but it takes a long time for them to make up their mind.

-Unpredictable, dramatic and secretive.

-Can withhold important information from others until it's too late for them to act on it. Can also change their mind at the last minute.

-Is very hard to read or get close to as they are always changing their emotions as soon as something new comes along or inspires them.

-Communicate well with all sorts of people, and are totally unpredictable in terms of wanting lots of money or not worrying about it at all.

-Very stubborn, and will be hard to convince otherwise of anything.

-Feel strongly about her beliefs and have no problem standing up for them.

-Can also be very critical at times because they are focused on the big picture instead of being petty.

Oprah was initially a public relations executive who abandoned her career during the mid-1980s for a live show that would be taped in Atlanta, Georgia. After gaining viewers in Chicago and Seattle, she began recording her show in 1986 in Chicago and moved her show permanently to Chicago after its successful first year there. In 1990, Oprah created the Oprah Winfrey Network (OWN), an American cable television network which features programming related to self-improvement, spirituality, health and entertainment.

Oprah Winfrey is an inspiration for people all over the world who want to create a better life for themselves. Her unique mix of drama, spirituality, healing and practical tips has resonated with viewers since 1986. Oprah has always been passionate about helping others reach their full potential and turn their lives around.

She's not only had a profound impact on her audience but also on the business world as well. Her success in broadcasting translated into success with other business interests like publishing, acting, production and film. Oprah has also created the O Foundation, the Oprah Winfrey Leadership Academy for Girls in South Africa and The Oprah Winfrey Leadership Academy for Girls in Georgia.

Her philanthropic efforts have been recognized by several groups and include a Presidential Medal of Freedom (2011), the French Legion of Honour, the Congressional Gold Medal, and honorary degrees from Harvard, Brown, Yale and Duke. Oprah's success has inspired many people to pursue their dreams and reach for the stars.

In 2017 she was awarded with an honor from the Academy Awards for her achievement in entertainment.

Chapter 2: What are Affirmations

Affirmations can be a powerful tool when it comes to breaking your bad habits for good. Saying affirmations is a great way to help you start changing negative thoughts and behaviors in a positive way. Affirmations are basically statements about the things you want in life, such as losing weight or improving your relationships. They show us what we want out of our lives, remind us of what we already have, and help us plan for what's coming next.

The key to successfully using affirmations is to make them personal. The more you can relate them to your own situations, the greater their impact. You should also avoid affirmations that can be interpreted negatively or imply you have or have not done something. For example, there is little point in telling yourself, "I'm a failure" as this statement does nothing except work at the subconscious level to reinforce failure in all areas of your life. A better statement would be: Today I made a mistake but I don't care; I know how to learn from my mistakes and I will do better next time.

This statement is positive and is aimed at finding a way to improve yourself instead of reinforcing negativity. In addition, say each affirmation every day. The most effective way to do this is by recording them on a CD or tape as opposed to repeating them out loud. Affirmations have a greater impact on us when we listen to them while we are in our relaxed state of mind, allowing the information to sink into our subconscious minds and change our behaviors accordingly.

Affirmations are a true gem in the world of self-improvement. Affirmations can work in a variety of ways, from simply spouting them aloud to writing them down on paper to even meditating with positive thoughts rattling around in your mind. Regardless of how you choose to use them, affirmations will help you focus on the good things about yourself and your life while simultaneously removing negative thinking that may be holding you back from success.

Affirmations can be a quick, easy way to shift your focus and improve your life, as long as you know how to use them effectively.

Affirmations are positive statements that are repeated to yourself in order to change the way you think about yourself and life in general. For example, if you're feeling frustrated with the lack of work available in your field and think that no job is out there for you, an affirmation could be "I am a hard worker and will find a job." Affirmations aren't hard and fast rules about what you should believe; rather, they're pep talks meant to boost your confidence. Affirmations can be repeated out loud, in your head or written down and stored somewhere. They can be anything that you want them to be, so long as they're positive and you truly believe in the message.

How Can Affirmations Help You?

Affirmations help by shifting the way you view yourself and life at large. When you repeat an affirmation over and over again, it will begin to seep into your subconscious, causing a shift in your beliefs about yourself. When this happens, you'll begin to think differently about your goals and the path you should take to achieve them. Instead of seeing things as impossible or out of reach, you'll start to feel more confident and in control. This will help motivate you to take action and make positive changes to your life that will improve your feeling of well-being.

Are There Any Affirmations I Should Not Use?

Affirmations are not meant to be used in place of traditional therapy or talk therapy sessions because they deal solely with the way one thinks about themselves. Using affirmations can actually make it harder to find a therapist or professional who can truly help if your problems run deeper than simply being unhappy with yourself or your life. If you think you need to see a therapist or counselor, do so.

Can I Affirm for Others?

You can use affirmations on other people, but the results may vary. If you have a friend who is extremely negative and keeps talking about how much better they had it "back in the day," you could use affirmations to try and get them to change their ways. However, just because someone else is speaking positive statements out loud doesn't mean they're truly believing them, which will keep them from having any positive effect on your life. Find out if someone else truly believes what they're saying before using affirmations on them so that you can accurately gauge whether or not they'll work for that person.

How to Use Affirmations Effectively

Using affirmations effectively is key to their success. Here are some tips on how to use them to their full potential.

Keep it positive: It's important that your affirmations are positive statements. If you say "I am not going to be late, I will be on time," or "I am capable of being healthy," then you're focusing on the negative and telling yourself what you're not rather than what you are or what you can do. This will cause your thoughts and feelings to shift in a negative direction, making your affirmations less effective. Instead of thinking "I am not going to be late, I will be on time," you need to try and think "I will arrive on time and stay on time." This will help shift your mindset from one that is negative to one that is positive, which is what you should want. Do this for everything in your life: The same thing goes for affirmations for your goals, either for yourself or someone else. Instead of saying "I will lose weight," you might think "I can eat healthy foods and stay active." You'll notice that instead of focusing on what you're not doing—weight loss—you'll focus on what you can do now. Instead of saying "I will be happy," think about how you can be happy. Find something that makes you smile or laugh and repeat it to yourself over and over again. It's a lot easier to think positively when you're feeling good about yourself, so take advantage of the positive moods you feel to help keep yourself optimistic.

Affirmations Are Worthwhile Tools in the Fight for Success

The best thing about affirmations is that they work, regardless of how long it takes for them to do so. Affirmations are meant to be a constant reminder that you can do anything you want and overcome any obstacle life throws at you. To keep this in mind, make sure you're repeating your affirmations regularly, 24 hours a day, 7 days a week. It won't help much if you only use them once a week or during the night when everything is quiet. Once your mind becomes used to hearing your affirmations and realizes that they're not going away anytime soon, it will begin to shift into the positive mindset they bring with them. You will start to believe that you can do anything you want and be the person you truly want to be.

Affirmations are one of the easiest methods to help change the way your mind thinks. To make them more effective, use them regularly and don't stress about trying to think of something that's positive in every single situation. Instead, try saying something to yourself that will focus on having faith in yourself, your knowledge or experience, or your ability to succeed. By focusing on what you have instead of what you don't, you'll bring a much deeper sense of confidence into your life and create a mindset that is more conducive for success.

Affirmations are little sentences that you repeat over and over, to help your subconscious mind accept them as true. Positive affirmations can be powerful tools for changing the way we feel, think and act.

We recommend following these guidelines: Eliminate any phrases that limit or negate yourself Like "I am not good enough" and "I am ugly". Cut the sentence in two Use only positive affirmations on both sides of the slash Like "I am beautiful"/"Some days I'm not." Use words that describe feelings that you want to experience like "peaceful" or "happy" as opposed to general descriptions like "funny".

Why You Should Do It

The subconscious mind takes in information, but doesn't understand language. When you repeat something to yourself over and over again, your subconscious is "trained" to accept it as true or real. So saying something like "I can't lose weight. I am just going to gain it all back" is not going to work very well because of that little word I. It doesn't define who you are, and you can always change who you are by changing your thoughts and behaviors. So say something like, "I am fit and healthy. My body is lean, strong and beautiful." Notice that you define the words you use – so the statement is much more empowering. To make it even better, associate specific emotions with the words – so it becomes a positive affirmation that makes you feel great on a deep level. For example:

"I love my body" or "My body is getting stronger every day" or "My legs are toned and taut, my abs are firm and flat – I am fit and healthy." Remember to use your best words for what you want to feel.

How To Use Them

The best way to use affirmations is by repeating them over and over again, for at least 15 minutes per day. Some people like to say their affirmations in the morning, before they get out of bed. Others like to say them at night, before they go to sleep. Find the time that works best for you and stick with it every day. It may be fun to have a little notebook or tape recorder with you so that you can jot down your favorite affirmations or make small recordings of yourself reading them aloud – so that you can listen later or share with others.

Some people like to have a notebook to jot down their favorite affirmations in. This can be a good idea if you want to make sure that you don't forget your favorite ones. If you do this, it is better not to write them down until after you have repeated them several times so that the words are more fully "stuck in your mind".

Say a positive affirmation every day, because it builds up and strengthens your mind-body connection and will become easier and easier to use as time goes on. Repeat the affirmation several seconds or minutes after the original statement – so that it gets imprinted in your brain. Repeat it again and again over the course of the day, especially if you encounter a setback or feel like you are relapsing into old, negative habits.

Does Afirmations Work

There is no such thing as a sure fire way to improve how you speak and think. However, affirmations, which are often referred to as positive mantras or wordy appeals to success, have long been debated as a possible tool for many kinds of self-improvement. Could they help increase your productivity? Improve your concentration? Remind you of the things you really want in life? Such questions have been asked by those who study affirmations for many years, but an answer was not readily forthcoming until recently.

The idea of affirmations has been around since at least the 1930s, and some people believe the idea is much older than that. Jacob LaMothe and Napoleon Hill both wrote on the subject, but it really wasn't until Louise L. Hay began writing about affirmations in 1975 that they gained popularity in popular media. Hay began writing after she was diagnosed with breast cancer and found that her own beliefs would not allow her to accept the notion of death; she found affirmation in both herself and those around her and turned those experiences into a book called "You Can Heal Your Life".

A few years later, Faye Dancer published an article about the process of making affirmations work for you. The article outlined several methods for putting affirmations to use in your everyday life and getting the most out of them. Here are a few of the things she said you can do:

– Be prepared if they don't work at first. In fact, be prepared that they may never seem to take hold…

-it is not necessary to believe in affirmations because we are familiar with their usefulness…

-start using them just as though they were some new invention. Be open to the results, no matter how strange or seemingly unbelievable the affirmations seem to you initially…

-experiment… now is your chance to put into practice what you have read about and heard about affirmations. Put them into everyday vocabulary and see how you like it… find out if they work for you or not.

-discover your own style of making affirmations work for you; experiment with different ways of using affirmations until you find one that works best for you. You may need to try a few before finding the one that clicks with your personality… Listen to other people's suggestions-but don't copy them or rely on someone else's judgment of whether they are working or not.

In subsequent years, many people have begun to suggest that one of the main benefits of affirmations is that they can help you better manage your self-esteem by helping you feel good about yourself and the way you are. As a result, affirmations are a very common form of self-help tool. The Internet has made them much more available to a wide variety of people who would like to put them to use for personal improvement, and some research has shown that affirmations seem to be working for many people.

They can certainly help increase your confidence, but have some drawbacks as well. The main one is that they seem very formulaic, which could mean that you may not put altogether much effort into them, or put them to use in a way that actually makes you feel better. In addition, affirmations don't work for everyone the same way; each person has different beliefs about what behaviors lead to happiness and self-improvement, so some people's affirmations will work a bit differently from your own.

Affirmations are certainly a great tool for positive thinking if you are willing to put forth some effort. While they aren't likely to make all your problems just disappear, they can at least get you more in touch with what you are thinking and how it may be affecting the rest of your life.

Chapter 3:   Morning Affirmations

The life of a Black women is not as easy as it seems — we face sexism, racism, and other types of discrimination on a daily basis. And while we spend countless hours working to break through these barriers and succeed in society, sometimes we need an extra little push to help us get up and go. That's why morning affirmations can help us start our day with positivity. Here are some affirmations for Black women that will make you feel great every morning!

"I deserve the best."

"Today is the first day of the rest of my life. Each day is a new beginning."

"Things will get better. I will continue to be the best version of myself."

"I am worth it."

"I will do my best today to lift up others, support myself, and make a difference."

"Today is the perfect day to both give and receive love."

"What makes me proud is that I know I can push through anything in life — even when people may doubt me — because of how strong Black Women are."

"I am more than enough. I am Black and beautiful."

"I will work harder than anyone else even when I feel like giving up!"

"I have the power to choose between being a victim or a survivor."

"Every time I learn from my mistakes, I become successful in life."

"My goal is to become an inspiration for others."

"The more blessings I have, the more opportunities I have to share with others."

""I can do hard things."

"I have to be my own best friend and encourage myself when I feel like giving up."

"I am not afraid to fail."

"Every time I am afraid of something, I will try it anyway."

"Every mistake is a lesson – and I learn from them."

"I will follow my dreams – no matter how far they take me."

""No matter what anyone else says or thinks of me, I know that I am beautiful in every way."

"Black Women can stick together, laugh together and love together. It doesn't matter what our skin tone or background might be."

"I am a strong and beautiful Black Woman."

"My spirit is beautiful, my roots are deep, my soul is wise and my will is indomitable."

"I will get it done!"

"What makes me proud is that I don't need anyone to tell me I can do it – because I know I can do anything."

"Curls, freckles, ebony skin and being from Africa is what makes me proud. It all goes to show that God made us all unique for a reason."

"I am a beautiful Black Woman."

"I am not what happened to me, I am what I choose to become."

"I will do my best to uphold the standards of Black Power."

"I will survive and thrive despite any obstacles in my life."

"I am not defined by my circumstances. When I rise above them, I will be a better person for it."

"Black Women are more than the way they look – they are intelligent and loving women with beauty in their hearts."

"I will avoid blaming others when I fail, and instead focus on how I can learn from my mistakes."

"I'm Black, and that's all I need to know."

"My smile is too bright for the world to ignore."

"Being a Black woman means that I must be mentally tough."

"Beauty is not skin deep – beauty is in the heart."

"While my skin may be dark it does not define me as a person or who I am as a woman".

"God saw you in your most vulnerable state and created something amazing with you. He placed you in the womb of a Black woman, to live and die as a Black woman. That is your purpose – to be a catalyst for change within our community, throughout the world and for people of all nations.. You are walking with purpose unmatched and unstoppable. Never forget that the world needs you and the world cries out for you. Your gift is your calling. When others see beauty they will be drawn to you and see within what we see in ourselves – beauty that transforms all who behold it with love. Your beauty is a gift that changes the world. Be courageous – be outspoken and be yourself. As Black Women we will rise up and look at ourselves in the mirror with pride. We will stop putting ourselves down and speak life into each other which is an indication of what we see in our own eyes."

"I am more than enough because I am a woman of God"

"I can do hard things."

"The more blessings I have, the more opportunities I have to share with others."

"I am not afraid to fail."

""No matter what anyone else says or thinks of me, I know that I am beautiful in every way."

"My purpose is to become an inspiration for others."

"I am beautiful, intelligent and loving in every way."

""No matter what happens to me in life, my people are always there for me."

"Being a Black woman means that I must be mentally tough."

""Black Girl Magic": What makes me proud is that I know I can push through anything in life — even when people may doubt me — because of how strong Black Women are."

""Be courageous – be outspoken and be yourself. As Black Women we will rise up and look at ourselves in the mirror with pride. We will stop putting ourselves down and speak life into each other which is an indication of what we see in our own eyes."

"I am more than great because I have a new beginning."

"My spirit is beautiful, my roots are deep, my soul is wise and my will is indomitable."

""No matter what happens to me in life, my people are always there for me.""

Chapter 4: Motivational Affirmations

Dismantling the same old notions about what being black means is not easy. It's often a struggle that is met with obstacles and uncertainty, but it is possible to change how people perceive us. One part of this process includes learning how to conduct ourselves through the lenses we were raised in-within our homes, schools, communities and society. If you want to be an agent of change then you need to first learn how these lenses work-what they are and why they exist in society today. There are also other ways that a person can fight against racism/white supremacy including building community while practicing radical acts of love towards yourself.

Even if you are in a position where you can't change the way your community functions you have the power to change yourself. It is through our daily actions and behaviors that we either grow or stagnate as people. This is why black women must take a stand and reclaim the notion of liberation from within our own communities-where it has always been. The following are some suggested motivational affirmations for black women to use throughout this process:

"I am Black."

"I am Determined."

"I will not allow frustrations to dictate my fate."

"The only way I stop being angry is by being loving and mindful towards myself. I will become more aware of my thoughts."

"I will not allow people to push negative messaging on me. I will take the time to examine and challenge the messages that I receive."

"I am brave."

"I will not fall victim to the dangers of victim-hood and proclaiming that I am a target of oppression because of the color of my skin."

"I am changing myself, the people around me and society through radical love toward myself and others."

"Radical love is a choice-a choice that I make every day by practicing radical acts of love toward myself, others, and society as a whole. It is a testament to the fact that I will always strive to be a better person and make this world a better place."

"I am powerful."

"I am responsible for how I conduct myself and the changes that I want to see in society."

"I will not allow my anger and frustrations to turn me into a victim. These feelings are only holding me back."

"I will remain hopeful by taking action-by practicing radical acts of love-within my community and the world at large."

"Even if it's one person, every act of self-love helps lead me closer to the life that I want. It's this idea that keeps me moving forward. I will keep running towards it until I get there."

"The color of my skin and the history surrounding black women hasn't defined me or my destiny. It's the choices that I make each day that will shape my life and legacy."

"I am in control of who I am and I can create an identity for myself without the crutch of other people's opinions."

"There are people out there who will see me as a threat because of the color of my skin-despite all the other positive things about me. This is why I must strive to be a role model for myself, instead of trying to win over anyone else's approval. It's this idea that I choose not to fight with people who only want to bring me down."

"I am Black. The color of my skin doesn't define me but it is an important part of who I am. I embrace my blackness by being proud of how far we have come and how far we are still willing to go. It's this pride that keeps me moving forward."

"There are people out there who will see me as a burden because they don't understand what it means to be Black in America. This is why I must strive to be the best person possible in order withstand the tests that life brings my way. It's this idea that I choose to stand strong and look towards a better tomorrow."

"I am Black. I am beautiful."

"I am a queen. There's a reason why others want me to be their queen because I'm a very rare person in the world who is genuinely good. It's this goodness that keeps me moving forward."

"Being nice to someone is radical love, but it must be done consciously, with purpose and without an ulterior motive. I will practice radical acts of love towards myself and others. It's this idea that keeps me moving forward."

"I am in control of my own destiny. I decide how life will treat me, how I will perceive the world, and how I will react to it. It's this idea that keeps me moving forward."

"I do not need to be validated by the opinions of others. The world is full of people who can't understand what it means to be Black in America. This is why I must strive to do more for myself and those around me so that I can influence positive change on a more global level. It's this idea that keeps me moving forward.

"For every thought I have about the world, if I'm not thinking about myself, I'm thinking about others-about how to make this world a better place for everyone. It's this idea that keeps me moving forward."

"I choose not to be a victim. To claim victim-hood is to release my power of control over myself and my life. I will build self-awareness in order to become someone who can problem solve instead of dwelling on the past or complaining about the here and now."

"I will continue to take action by being loving and mindful towards those within my community and society at large. It's this idea that keeps me moving forward. I am in control of overcoming the challenges that life has placed in front of me. It's me against the world. In the end, it doesn't matter how many people are against me, I will find a way to win."

"My Blackness means more to me than other people's opinions about it. The color of my skin is an important part of who I am and has shaped my life for the better. Even though there are people who don't understand why I am entitled to say that I'm Black, this is why I must strive to do everything in my power to ensure that we can all come together as a community despite our differences. It's this idea that keeps me moving forward."

"I am Black. I am beautiful. I am powerful."

This is how I reclaim my power and build self-esteem by transforming myself into a queen, who checks the thoughts and attitudes of others in order to become unaffectable. It's this idea that keeps me moving forward."

"I will continue to take action by practicing radical acts of love with the people around me. It's this desire that keeps me moving forward."

"My life is meant to be an example of what it means to be Black in America. It's this reason why I must strive to do more for others than anyone else ever has. I want people to know that my life is not only about me but also about the future generations to come. It's this idea that keeps me moving forward."

"I will take action by educating myself and others. It's this idea that keeps me moving forward."

"Whether it's one person or everyone, everyone matters and does play a role in how I view the world. The size of my impact depends on my level of consciousness. It's this idea that keeps me moving forward."

"I am proud to be Black because I have been given many gifts in life so that I can give back to the world by using them as tools for good and toward creating a better future for all of us. It's this idea that keeps me moving forward."

"I will take action by being and doing better than anyone ever has. It's this idea that keeps me moving forward."

"My Blackness is a part of me that I'm not trying to hide. The color of my skin isn't a flaw, but it's an important part of who I am. I embrace my blackness by being proud of how far we have come and how far we are still willing to go. It's this pride that keeps me moving forward."

"There are people out there who will see my success as a threat because they're not used to seeing someone like me win in life. This is why I must strive to be the best person possible in order withstand the tests that life brings my way. It's this idea that I choose to stand strong and look towards a better tomorrow."

"I am Black. I am both Black and woman, which means that twice as many people are trying to take me down. This is why I must strive to be twice as good as the next person so that I can prove to myself and others that we are still here, despite everything stacked against us. It's this idea that keeps me moving forward."

"I will practice radical acts of love towards myself and others at all times because there are people out there who only want me to fail in life. It's this idea that keeps me moving forward."

"I am in control of my own destiny. I decide how life will treat me, how I will perceive the world, and how I will react to it. Even though people may not want to acknowledge the importance of being disciplined, it's this discipline that has gotten me this far in life. It's this idea that keeps me moving forward."

"I do not need to be validated by the opinions of others because I know firsthand what it feels like when people think that you are only good for one thing. I have done this to myself and others for far too long. It's this idea that keeps me moving forward."

"I am fully aware of the fact that I am Black and therefore carry a huge responsibility towards society. It is my responsibility to make sure that I take actions as a Black woman who leads by example in order to influence positive change in every facet of my everyday life. It's this idea that keeps me moving forward."

"I choose not to be a victim by claiming victim-hood. To claim victim-hood is to release control over my own life and let others determine the way in which I live mine. I will build self-awareness in order to become someone who can problem solve instead of dwelling on the past or complaining about the here and now."

"In life, there will always be people who want me to fail, but I am not going to let them win. It's this idea that keeps me moving forward."

"There are times when I will come face-to-face with people who do not understand my Blackness and how it affects the way in which I live my life. The thing is, I choose not to explain myself because 1) it's none of their business and 2) my Blackness isn't for them; it's for me. It's this idea that keeps me moving forward.

"I will take action by finding peace within myself and moving through life with grace. It's this idea that keeps me moving forward."

"My Blackness is not something that I can change. It's in my DNA and therefore it isn't going anywhere no matter how hard I try to hide it. The easiest thing to do is accept my blackness and learn how to embrace all of the good that comes with being Black in America; especially since I know firsthand the many downsides of being African American. It's this idea that keeps me moving forward."

"I will take action by smiling each and every day regardless of what is going on in my life. It's this idea that keeps me moving forward."

"I am proud to be Black because I love who I have become despite the many obstacles put in my way. It's this idea that keeps me moving forward."

"Seizing my blackness means that I can learn how to handle things differently, even if it means starting over again. It also means that I must conquer my fears and take action in order to move towards a better tomorrow because there are so many Black men and women who are dealing with their own fears whereas I have the ability to change what's going on around me. It's this idea that keeps me moving forward.

"My Blackness gives me the tools and knowledge needed to triumph in life. It's this idea that keeps me moving forward."

"Being a Black woman is both a blessing and a curse so I must remain focused at all times. There will always be people who want to bring me down because they think they can get away with it but I'm not going to let them steal my joy. I am Black and proud! It's this idea that keeps me moving forward.

"I will take action by feeding myself the proper information that I need in order to make better decisions in life. By being a Black woman who is historically aware, I become empowered to do great things because I know my history and what it takes to overcome the obstacles that Black people have faced throughout time. It's this idea that keeps me moving forward."

"All of us want to be loved unconditionally but the reality is that we must earn love by loving ourselves first and proving to everyone else that we are worthy of getting our love and respect through hard work and dedication. It's this idea that keeps me moving forward."

"I will take action by avoiding people who have been placed in my life to distract it from the goals and dreams I have for myself. It's this idea that keeps me moving forward."

"I will take action by keeping my eyes open for the next great opportunity in life. I will remain focused on taking my current talents and skills to the next level by following my passion, doing what I love to do and not allowing anyone or any situation to stop me from doing so. It's this idea that keeps me moving forward."

"The ability to set and achieve goals regardless of the hardships I face is what makes me different from everyone else. It's this idea that keeps me moving forward."

"To seize my blackness means that I am ready for any obstacles that come my way because I have learned how to use obstacles as a tool towards growth and development. It's this idea that keeps me moving forward."

"I will take action by letting go of the past and place all of my energy into the present, because the very moment I waste my time thinking about what has happened in the past, it makes it difficult for me to be in the moment and move forward. It's this idea that keeps me moving forward."

"I know I have a lot to offer but I must work hard in order to realize how valuable I am to myself and others. It's this idea that keeps me moving forward."

"I love who I am . . . Black, strong, confident and proud! It's this idea that keeps me moving forward.

"I will take action by letting go of people who do not support me and focusing my energy on the people who do. It's this idea that keeps me moving forward."

"My Blackness is a blessing in disguise because it has helped me obtain what I have a right to; freedom, love and respect. I refuse to remain distanced from the greatness that is being Black because I am a Black woman and there are too many of us with our own unique stories to tell. It's this idea that keeps me moving forward."

"As for myself, I refuse to let anyone or anything stop my drive towards greatness because I will never stop trying until I achieve the success that is rightfully mine. It's this idea that keeps me moving forward."

"As for myself, I will take action by making sure that everyone around me acknowledges my greatness whenever they see me. It's this idea that keeps me moving forward."

"My blackness is a blessing in disguise because it has helped me obtain what I have a right to; freedom, love and respect. I refuse to remain distanced from the greatness that is being Black because I am a Black woman and there are too many of us with our own unique stories to tell. It's this idea that keeps me moving forward."

"I will take action by making sure that everyone around me knows that I am a Black woman who is confident and proud of who she is. It's this idea that keeps me moving forward."

"My blackness is a source of power which comes from within, and is nurtured by the multiple experiences I've had in my life. It's this idea that makes me move forward.

"My blackness gives me the tools and knowledge needed to triumph in life. It's this idea that keeps me moving forward."

"Being a Black woman is both a blessing and a curse so I must remain focused at all times. It's this idea that keeps me moving forward."

"I will take action by not allowing myself to get discouraged when challenges arise in life. It's this idea that keeps me moving forward."

"I am a Black woman who is ready to seize her Blackness in order to make a positive change in the world. It's never too late to work towards making my life better so I will continue doing just that because I refuse to allow anyone or anything stop me from becoming the person I need and want to be. It's this idea that keeps me moving forward.

Chapter 5:   Leadership Affirmations

A list of affirmations to remind yourself just how amazing you are in every facet of life. Whether it is a list of affirmations for black women to remind them they are beautiful and successful, or a list for women who may feel like they need an extra boost to keep going strong, these affirmations will help you find strength and motivation:

- You're beautiful and wonderful in every way.

- Your confidence shines through.

- You believe in yourself.

- Therefore, what is there for me not to believe in you?

- You're the best person I know.

- I've got your back!

- Everything is yours.

- You're capable, beautiful and brilliant.

- You are more than enough.

- You're an original.

- You're wonderful, beautiful, kind and amazing in every way.

- It's all about you! That's why I love you so much!

- Worship yourself and never stop!

 - Your smile is contagious!

- When your confidence shines through, everything around you begins to change for the better.

- You're fierce, and you're not afraid to take on the world!

- Good things come to those who believe in themselves. Be a believer!

- You are worthy of all the wonderful things that life has to offer.

- You can do whatever you set your mind to.

- It's alright if others don't see what I see in you; they are just missing out on how awesome you truly are.

- There will always be someone who sees your potential, and there will always be situations where you have no choice but to trust yourself. Do just that.

- I know you can do it! #blackwomenaremagic

- You are meant for greatness.

- When you're feeling down, go back to the person you know you really are; the person who never doubts their self worth, the one who loves and trusts themselves completely. That is who I love, and all of that is why I believe in your power and strength.

- Just believe in yourself!

- With anyone else, I would have given up long ago; but with you, I know there is always a chance to make things better.

- You are my best friend and it's because of that amazing quality that I know you will succeed in whatever you put your mind to.

- You're the greatest person I know, and I just want to thank you for being such an encouraging source of strength. I love you.

- You can make it through any situation, no matter how challenging it may seem. You've overcome so much already, there is no way that anything else could get the best of you!

- You're a tremendous person and there's no way anyone could not love you just the way you are.

- There is no one who hasn't set their eyes on you and fallen in love with your inner beauty. You've become a beacon for all to see.

- Even though others may not acknowledge it, I can always look at myself and say: "She's amazing."

- You're so talented; everyone should know about it.

- People may try to break you down, but your spirit can't be crushed by anyone. Keep going!

- Be proud of who you are and what you do; never give up on yourself.

- When you're down, remember all of the times where I was able to pick you up when no one else would. Remember how I always said, "You are enough."

- When you feel alone, just look inside and you will see me on the inside.

- You are a rare jewel for everyone to hold onto; never let go.

- My love for you is like an ocean, never ending; when others are trying to destroy parts of your life just because they don't understand who you are as a person, I believe in all of the wonderful qualities that lie deep within your soul.

- You're a wonderful friend and there's no one I'd rather have by my side through a difficult time in life.

- Everyone wants to tear down someone else's confidence, but it's most important to keep your own.

- You have a beautiful soul that shines through everything you do and say.

- You're capable, beautiful and brilliant.

- If you haven't been told it already, I just want to let you know that I am always here for you whenever you need someone to lift up your spirits.

- You're wonderful, beautiful, kind and amazing in every way.

- Reflect back on your accomplishments; if you need encouragement, all you have to do is think about them, and I know for a fact that all will become clear.

 - "I am enough.

- You're a tremendous friend and there's no one I'd rather have by my side through a difficult time in life.

- There was nobody else so compassionate, caring and kind as she was. She was very much loved.

- You've been through so much already, you have nothing to worry about.

- I believe in you!

- You are capable, beautiful, brilliant and kind.

- I know you have it in you to be a success as long as you keep believing in yourself and don't let any obstacles stand in your way.

- When things get tough and the feeling of doubt creeps in, remember that it's always going to be me who stands by your side, encouraging you to continue on with your dreams.

- I love you, and that's why I'll always be there for you when things get tough.

- You never have to doubt yourself because there is nobody else who has your back like I do.

- Whenever life seems tough, think back on all of your accomplishments and remember that there's no way anything could ever stand in the way of your goals.

- There is always a bright side to looking back at your life and remembering all of the wonderful times you've had with your friends and family.

- I know that whatever you need from me, I'll be there for you.

- I wish that everyone could see the beauty inside of you, but most importantly I wish that you would see it too.

- You're always going to be the one who lights up the room with your smile and makes everyone feel happier, especially when they're around you.

- When you feel down and like you need some cheering up, just remember that within yourself lies all of the qualities needed to make anyone's day better.

- When the time is right, the world will see exactly how amazing you are.

- Your beauty radiates from within.

- With each passing day Facebook community is more active than there was before .

- People with Myspace account are becoming more active and join Facebook group.

- I support my friend to be the first black woman in Manhattan to get a degree from an Ivy League University;

- I want a career as an actress because I love acting and I think everyone should be able to experience that passion.

- I want to be the first black woman in Manhattan to get a degree from an Ivy League University;

- I want to see the first black woman receive a doctorate from Harvard, attend Yale and Columbia, become vice president at NBC, produce film at Fox, and weather forecaster at Fox's WFLA.

- When I grow up, I want to do some of the things that Oprah has done in her lifetime.

- TV is a great way to make a name for yourself as long as you know how it works; you have to promote yourself.

- You are the light of the world.

- There is always a bright side to looking back at your life and remembering all of the wonderful times you've had with your friends, family and supporters.

Chapter 6:   Healing Affirmations

Affirmations are a powerful way to help you reshape your thoughts and improve your outlook. By repeating them, you can change the way you think about yourself and transform difficult experiences into triumphs.

In our culture, black women have been taught to constantly keep up with strength in order to combat racism, sexism, oppression and other forms of discrimination. Unfortunately, this is often accomplished through threats of violence or harming the men who oppose them. This behavior doesn't help anyone heal or move forward; it only perpetuates pain and suffering in the long run.

Instead, we should use affirmations to work on our inner selves and conquer the contradictions that keep us from moving forward.

If you're a black woman and want to use affirmations for positive purposes, you can use my list of healing affirmations for black women as a guide. While these specific affirmations may not apply to you, the general concepts are universal and can be used in similar contexts.

"I let go of all my pain, anger, and stress." This affirmation is very general because everyone has different experiences with each of these feelings. For example, some black women hold onto pain because it helps them understand what they've overcome in life. On the other hand, some black women are so angry about the things that have happened to them that it becomes a burden. You can personalize this affirmation by addressing what you're holding onto, be that pain, anger or stress.

"Every night I will open up to someone with kind and compassionate words." This could be a family member, friend or even a professional counselor. It's important to get these feelings out of your chest so you can move forward in everyday life.

"I am valued and respected in this world." Racism can often make black women feel unwanted, but that doesn't need to be the case. In some instances, the treatment of black women is dehumanizing and downright cruel; however, that's not true for all races (especially whites). Keep in mind that the actions of one do not define an entire group, so don't let those actions dictate how you think about yourself.

"I am an island, and I am surrounded by wonderful people." By saying this, you acknowledge that you can bounce back from negative experiences. Just because someone treats you poorly doesn't mean that it will happen all the time; maybe they had a bad day. In order to keep moving forward, you need to remember that there are many good people who share your beliefs and are looking out for your best interests.

"I have worth and I deserve respect." You have value in this world, so always work toward showing yourself some love. You don't need to be perfect, but you do need to work toward being all that you can be.

"I am a beautiful and amazing person." You can sometimes feel like this statement is untrue and that the universe is conspiring against you. By saying this affirmation, however, you'll realize that the bad things in life are not a reflection of who you are as a person. Instead, it shows what's happening in your life and how others treat black women in general.

"I am full of power, knowledge and strength."

"I have compassion for everyone around me."

"I know my worth. I am not a victim." Just because something bad has happened to you doesn't mean that you have to accept it as part of your life; however, you can't let it rule your entire existence.

"My life is in my hands and I will use it wisely." This affirmation shows that you need to be wise when making decisions if want to live a happy and fulfilling life. Always work toward building a foundation of positivity so that your options are endless.

"I am always learning how to love myself." There are many different ways to show love, but the best way is by loving yourself. In the long run, this is the best gift you can give yourself and those around you.

"I have the power to heal past wounds and forgive those who have caused me pain." This is another very general affirmation; however, you can personalize it by addressing what's causing you pain and what you wish to forgive. For example, do you want to forgive someone who wronged you or does forgiveness mean that you're willing to forget about it? While it's not easy to let go of these emotions, using affirmations is one way that helps us cope with these feelings and move on.

"I am an eternal being, a flame of life burning brightly and illuminating this world." You can't let anything stop your path on life and if something has happened in your past, never lose hope. This is the most important affirmation to use when you're feeling ready to let go of negative emotions.

"I will not be held back by the past." You can't change the past, so instead of allowing it to keep you down, instead work toward moving forward in a positive manner.

"I am so much more than I ever thought I could be." We often feel small and insignificant, but you're much more than what others think about you. Sometimes people treat us poorly just because of their own insecurities; however, you can remind yourself that there's always time for growth and enlightenment.

"I have nothing to prove to anyone. I am a shining star." This affirmation helps you to remember that you do not have to prove yourself to anyone else and that your talents are not just for show. Instead, they can be used toward helping others and bringing your gifts to the forefront.

"I have limitless potential." No matter where you are in life, you're always working toward achieving something; however, don't limit how far you can go.

"I am so much more than what I see in the mirror." You might feel like you're not pretty enough, have a "bad hair day" or that there's something wrong with your appearance. However, you are much more than what others see on the outside.

"I am perfectly imperfect." Being perfectly imperfect is the most beautiful thing in the world because it means you're human. Everyone has their flaws and our appearance can't be perfect; instead, we can focus on being happy and loving ourselves for what we are.

"I'm an old soul." This is another one of those affirmations that helps you to remember how far along you've already been in life. It's important that you recognize how old you are, but also remind yourself of your younger days.

"I am a child of the universe." You might feel like an outsider at times and you might feel unsure about where you're heading on life. However, it's important to remember that this too is part of the journey. You're always just learning more about yourself, so don't stress over where life is headed.

"I can let go of my fears and I am safe." We all have fears, but it's important to know that these fears can be defeated or conquered. Instead of allowing them to stop us from reaching our goals, instead use affirmations to conquer your feelings.

"I am the creator of my life." This is a very important affirmation because it helps you to believe in yourself and the power that you have over your own destiny.

"I know I am enough." This is another great affirmation for those who feel like they're missing something or need more than what they're already receiving. It's always exciting when you can find out where to next step, but sometimes we don't know what we're meant to do or how we'll get there.

"I am grateful for everything." No matter how much you have in life, you can always find something more important to be grateful for.

"When I am ready, I know exactly how to go about it." This is a great affirmation that tells you that if certain situations arise in your life; there are ways that you can work toward resolving them. While some things might not seem as though they have an answer right away, many times by trusting yourself and allowing yourself the time to figure out the solution is all that's necessary.

"I am ready. I can do this." Many times, people encounter a situation that they feel is too big for them to handle and are afraid to take action. This affirmation reminds you that you're strong enough to overcome any challenge. You're not alone on this journey and no matter how big things seem, it's important to remember that it's just a choice away from being all better.

"I am safe." We all make mistakes or fall down in life, but then we get back up again and we can all move forward together.

"I have everything I need to succeed." Many people feel like they're missing something that they need in order to make their dreams come true. While everything might not be officially listed on your wish list, you can still find ways to make your dreams come true. You might struggle a little along the way, but with all that you've been through and all that you've learned, it's safe to say that there's nothing standing in the way of success for you.

"I am wonderful just as I am." This is a great affirmation which reminds us that we're already perfect just as we are today. We're doing our best and it's not a bad thing to be the man or woman you want to be. Even though you may not feel amazing, you're still beautiful.

"I am free from my past so I can move forward." We're all human and we're all going to make mistakes in life. You may have made some decisions that have changed your life or affected other people that's important to you. It's fine, but at the same time it's important to remember that your past is no longer overbearing on you. By owning your mistakes and taking responsibility for them, you can begin moving forward in a positive way toward who you want to be.

"I am never alone. I am never afraid." This is a great affirmation because it reminds you that in every instance, there is always someone that you can reach out and contact if you need help. You might be in an overwhelming situation or not know how to get through it, but by reaching out and communicating with others, you can help each other find solutions.

"I am calm and centered. I am at peace."

"I am calm and centered and I am at peace." This affirmation can be recited throughout the day to remind you that underneath all the chaos there's a sense of balance and serenity waiting for you inside. You deserve to feel happy and relaxed each day, so try reciting this affirmation whenever you're feeling tense or stressed out.

"I am a happy man." You deserve to be happy and if you're not happy, then you need to find what makes you happy. This affirmation will remind you of all the things that will keep you smiling from ear to ear. Whether it's a nice family dinner or a day with your friends, there's always something that can help lift your spirits.

"I have plenty of time." Time is one thing we never seem to have enough of and while things may seem like they're taking forever, know that there are always ways in which you can get things done quicker. The best part about this affirmation is that it reminds us to slow down and enjoy the moment instead of worrying about the future.

"I am happy." By surrounding yourself in positive and uplifting energy, you'll find that you have a larger sense of happiness throughout your life. There will always be tough moments and days where you feel down, but make a goal to stay positive for longer periods of time and focus on all the things you're grateful for.

"I am open to receive." When you're willing to accept the good things in life, they'll come much faster and much easier. By receiving all the joy and happiness others have to offer, you'll always have plenty of love in your life.

"I am grateful." This affirmation will help remind you of all the small things in life which make us happiest. Pay attention to the little things like sunshine, birds singing, nice smelling flowers, and good people who are around you. Even if you're in an overwhelming situation, there's always something for which to be thankful. This will help keep things in perspective.

"I enjoy my life." This is a great affirmation to say at the beginning of your day or even when you wake up in the middle of the night because it reminds you that your life is important and that you should never forget how blessed you are to have been given another day to live.

"I am successful. I am making my dreams come true."

"I have a vision of who I want to be and what I want to do." This is a great affirmation because it reminds us that we shouldn't always settle for anything less than our goals or dreams. It's fun to dream of traveling the world or getting married one day, but if you don't make those dreams a reality, then they'll never become yours.

"I know exactly what I want and I am willing to work for it." This is a wonderful affirmation because it will help you not get discouraged if things don't go your way. The best thing you can try to remember is that something out of the ordinary is just right in front of you and no matter what, you're going to have to work hard for it.

"I am prepared." "I have all the tools necessary to overcome any challenge that life might throw at me." You may never be able to predict all the challenges life will throw at you, but by taking time out each day, exercising and getting proper nutrition, these are things which will help keep you happy while keeping your body healthy as well.

"I deserve only the best." Never settle for anything less in life because you always deserve to have and do the best. Even if others aren't trying to give you their best, simply focus on what's important to you and always look for ways in which you can improve.

"I am allowing myself to be happy. I am willing to feel good about myself." The more you're willing to accept being happy inside, the wider the smile will be on your face.

"I look forward to every day of my life." This one is a great affirmation to say before you go to sleep or anytime throughout the day when you have some free time. By reading positive news or hearing positive things from others which can help put a smile on your face, you'll be able to wake up each morning with a sense of enthusiasm and joy.

"I will accept all that comes my way and make the best of it. Life is filled with ups and downs, but I will always hold onto the things which bring me joy." When you know that life can be challenging at times, it's easy for the bad to overshadow all of the good.

"I let go of all fear." "I am not afraid of anything in my life." The more you try to stay away from fear, the more it'll follow you around and haunt your thoughts. The fact is, you have to face your fears sooner or later, so why not just let them go and accept the fact that there are things in life which are out of your control.

"I do what I love." "I am willing to do what makes me happy and fulfill my life." When you're making the choice to do what you love, there's no way that you'll ever feel unhappy because it doesn't really matter how well or poorly a job goes if it's something which makes you happy. What's important is that you're doing something which lights up your soul.

"I always treat people with respect." Always remember that there are people in this world which are willing to help you and take care of you, and if it's a friend or loved one, they're going to want to be treated well as well.

"I choose to live without regret." "I am happy with the life that I have," "What I do today will determine my life later on."

"I have faith in myself. I know that I can do anything I put my mind to."

"I am seeking out my passions." "I am finding out what I love and enjoying every bit of doing it." There's no way that a person can truly be happy if they're doing something they don't really enjoy. That's why it's important for you to seek out your passions and do them on a regular basis. When you figure out what makes you happy, nothing can ever take that away from you.

"Today, I learned something new." "I will not repeat the same mistakes twice." The more mistakes you make in life, the more lessons you learn from them. By taking time each day to learn a little something new, it'll be easier for you to keep an open mind about things in this world and try to stay away from making the same mistakes over and over again.

"I am willing to change my ways." "I am willing to give up what is bad for me. I am willing to accept change." There are times in life when we may feel stuck in a rut and just simply won't be able to move forward until we find a way out. However, by being willing to change your ways and do things differently, you will always find a way to feel good about yourself again.

"I am worthy of happiness." "I will behave in ways which can bring me joy and fulfillment." "I have something good within me that keeps me going each day. I am the one who keeps myself looking up instead of down." "If I don't like my situation, then I must change it. I am in control of my life." As much as you want to be happy, by not caring what others may say or think about you, you'll always find a way to be happy.

"I am encouraging myself every day." "I know that I will accomplish whatever I choose to do." You may feel like people are discouraging you from doing anything or staying where you are in life, but it's important for the person trying to encourage them to remember that the person being encouraged is also doing the same thing. The more encouragement each one of us gives to ourselves, the easier it will be for us to succeed and help others as well.

"I let myself be guided by my inner voice. My wisdom and inner peace will always guide me in the right direction." When you listen to your inner voice, it will always help you make the choice to do what's best for yourself. The more you try to be told what to do as opposed to listening to your inner voice, the easier it will be for you to get stuck in habits and make mistakes.

"Every day is a new beginning." "I am using this morning as my new beginning." Each morning is a new chance at starting over. Whether you have something which happened yesterday or something that is about to happen tomorrow, it's important for you to learn from them and move on in the same way that yesterday ended. Every minute spent being negative is one less minute which you can spend doing what makes you happy.

"I am only out of control if I think I am." When you're making the choice to feel good about yourself, it's possible for things to still go wrong on the outside but your confidence remains strong within. If you're not worrying about things on the outside going wrong, then it's much easier for that bad feeling inside of you to disappear.

"I am seeking out my dreams. I am not afraid to follow my heart." If you want to find happiness, it's important for you to make sure you're not holding yourself back from following your dreams and following the path that leads you out of your comfort zone. By following your heart and doing things which excite you, you'll always be able to feel good about yourself.

"I will handle every situation as if it is a miracle, because every day is a miracle." We all have an opportunity at any given moment in life to do something which will help us feel good about ourselves. If you're going through a hard time or are in the middle of something challenging, it can be easy to give up or feel low about yourself. However, there's always an opportunity to turn this around.

"I am doing my best. I know that I can only be the best as much as I can." You're not always going to be able to do everything perfectly, but that doesn't mean you failed at something. It simply means that you did the best you could for that particular moment in time and helped others along the way.

"I am deserving of love." "I deserve happiness in my life." When you're feeling alone, it can be easy for you to lose sight of what makes you happy and what helps bring you joy. Try to take the time each day to focus on what makes you happy and make sure your happiness comes first.

"Under no circumstances will I let myself be ruled by fear or doubt." We're all afraid of making mistakes at some point because it can be easy for us to mentally get stuck in ruts which we don't know how to escape from. If we allow ourselves to follow our fears and negative thinking, then we'll never be able to do anything positive anymore. Luckily, you can change that by simply acknowledging that your fears aren't going to hurt anyone.

"I am worthy of being happy." "I deserve companionship, love and a home which is filled with laughter. There are many times in our lives when we believe we're not special or good enough, but the truth is that we're all deserving of being happy and following our dreams. By encouraging ourselves to reach for the things we want and not settling for less than what we deserve, it will help us feel good about ourselves each day.

"I will attempt to give something back to this world every day." "I am here right now, right where I need to be, in order for me to make all my dreams come true. I am doing this for myself, not for others, but because I want to make my life a better place for everyone who follows in my footsteps.

I may never get all the things I want before I die, but by giving back to this world every day, that might change." By keeping focused on your goals and the things you have to give back to the world, it will help you feel better about yourself.

"I am here for a reason." "I will continue living until I accomplish more than what I thought imaginable." Be encouraged that you're living right now at exactly the right time in order for something amazing someday. By the end of your life, you may not be able to accomplish everything that you want to do before it's time for you to move on, but don't give up. If there is anything special about you which allows you to do more than anyone else would be able to accomplish, then use that ability in order for others to benefit from your efforts.

"I am trying my best." The biggest regret someone will ever have in their life is living the rest of their life fearing that they've done something wrong. Don't spend a lot of time worrying about things which happened in your past because they're no longer affecting you now. Instead, make sure you're doing the best that you can in order for you to never have to worry about your past when you're too old to change anything.

"I am focusing on the opportunities which are being presented to me." "I am using my imagination in order to visualize what it will be like." A lot of times when people feel depressed or anxious, they begin worrying about things which haven't evenoccurred yet. This often results in them thinking that none of their goals are ever going to become a reality and they're going to be stuck in a life of unhappiness and regret.

"I am only going to focus on the good things in my life." "I am only going to speak about the things which are worth speaking about." Take the time each day to focus on all of the good things in your life instead of focusing on all of the bad things. By doing this, you're telling your mind that there are certainly more positive things in your life than negative ones and it will greatly boost your self-esteem.

"I deserve to be surrounded by good people." "Everything I do or say today is making a difference." "I am changing my life for better or for worse. I am either getting better or I am getting worse." We're all surrounded by good and bad people every day. However, instead of focusing on the negative people in our lives, we should always try to focus on the positive ones. Unless you're actively trying to do something which will make others happy, then you're probably not doing enough to make a difference in their life.

"I am living my dreams." "I am going after what I wish for everyday. I am making this happen and nothing is going to stop me." We all have goals which we wish would come true but we don't often have the determination or courage required to make them replace reality. However, by staying focused on your dreams and how you're going to make your life happier, it will make your dreams come true.

"I am doing what I want to do in my life." "I am living for me and not for others." "I am going after it all and I'm not stopping until I finally get there." It can be easy for you to focus on the things which other people are doing in order for you to feel bad. If they're making more money than you, then it can be easy for you to feel bad about yourself. However, you shouldn't let other people's actions affect your life on a daily basis. Instead, make it a point to do what you want to do in your life, have fun and enjoy life because that is what's going to allow you to feel good about yourself.

"I am at peace with myself." "I am grateful for all of my gifts." "I am thankful for each of the things which I have been given." Just like anything else, we can become unhappy if we don't recognize the things in our lives which are important and which we should be thankful for. By simply realizing this fact, you can start feeling better about yourself.

"I will surround myself with positive people. I will surround myself with happiness. I am grateful for what I have." "I am happy with the person I am today." "I will do something which benefits others every day." "I have everything I need in my life already. There is nothing else for me to be unhappy about. It is time for me to be at peace with myself and my life." This might be the most important one of all because it reminds you that no matter how bad your life may seem, you should always stay positive. By surrounding yourself with other positive people and by realizing that you have everything you need in order to live a happy life, it'll help make you feel better about yourself and your future.

"I am in control of my life." "I am in control of my destiny." "I refuse to let anything else affect me. I'll wake up today and choose happiness instead of unhappiness. I will make a difference in the lives of others every day." You can't change other people's problems but the only thing you can change about yourself is your own attitude. By believing that you have the power to change your own life, it will empower you and make it easier to take charge of your future. By making this change, it'll help you feel better about yourself and give you more confidence when interacting with others on a daily basis.

"My life is special. I am special. I can do anything I wish for." "I will not let anyone else control my thoughts, my actions or my life. I am in charge of everything which happens to me and in control of my future. It is my decision whether or not I will let negativity affect me. There is no reason for me to feel this way anymore." No matter how bad your life may seem, you always have the power to change it if you're willing to put forth the effort and determination required. By believing that you're special and that there's nothing you can't accomplish, it'll help make it easier for your dreams to come true one day.

"I have a right to be happy too. I don't deserve to be treated in a negative manner. I will not let their negativity affect me anymore." "I am not going to be afraid of the world around me anymore. It is time for me to get out there and enjoy my life to the fullest." We all have the right to be happy and we should never have to deal with negativity in any form throughout our lives. By deciding that you won't let other people's negativity affect you anymore and by realizing that you deserve to live a happy life, it'll make it easier for you to avoid letting other people down or disappointing them.

"I will always keep a positive attitude in life no matter what happens. I will always have a good outlook on life no matter what happens." "Today is the first day of the rest of my life. Today is a day for me to be grateful for everything that I have. Today is a day for me to live up to my full potential." No matter how bad your life may seem, you can always keep a positive attitude and choose to be happy no matter what happens. By doing this, you'll discover that it's much easier for you to deal with your problems on a daily basis and it'll certainly allow you to live the happy, successful life which you deserve.

"I am a survivor. I have learned from all of my past mistakes and I will not make the same ones again." "I have something to live for. I have something more important to accomplish than anything else, even my own happiness. I will not lose my motivation and focus until it is completed." One problem which most people experience is that once their goals are fulfilled, they seem to stop being positive about the future and become more defeated than ever before. By realizing that you still have things which you can accomplish in life, you'll be able to continue being happy while at the same time achieving your goals.

"I've been through enough already so I don't need any more of it. I don't need to prove anything to anyone, including myself. I do what I do for myself and for my own reasons." "Today is a new day. Today is the day when I finally get to live the life which I deserve. Today is the day in which I am going after everything that I wish for and nothing will stop me from getting there." No matter how bad you might think your life has been up until this point, realize that it's all in the past now and you can move on with your future no matter what happens. The more positive you become, the easier it'll be to let go of your bad experiences and allow yourself to start a new life which is full of happiness and prosperity.

"I am wiser now than I was yesterday and I will use the knowledge I have gained in life to make the decisions that suit me best." "Today, I am going to be wise. Today, I am going to learn about my own strengths and weaknesses." "I will not be afraid anymore. Today, I will not allow anything or anyone else's unhappiness affect me." "Today, every word which comes out of my mouth means something. I am going to make the right decisions so that my words can have a positive impact on others." By realizing that you learn from everything you've been through in life and by understanding that you're wiser now than you ever were before, it'll help make you feel better about yourself and your future. It makes it easier for you to make the best decisions possible without feeling like anything else is required from you.

"I will always be honest with myself and others. I will never do anything which goes against my own morals."

"My choices are mine and no one else's. I'm responsible for everything which happens to me."

"Today is a day when I get to live up to my full potential. Today is a day when I choose to be happy and I'm going to live life up to my full potential." No matter how bad something may seem in your life, you always have the power to make a positive change and you can live a life of happiness no matter what situation you're currently in. By deciding that honesty with yourself and those around you is important, it'll help make it easier for you to reach your goals without the need for deceit.

"I will have everything in my life which I need or want. I will never have anything which I don't need or want." The ability for us all to have whatever we desire is something which we all should strive for. By realizing that you deserve all of the things which you can possibly want and by making it easier for yourself to have them, you'll find it much easier to accomplish your goals and live a happy life.

"If I am not satisfied with what I have, I will make changes. If I reach a point in life where I am happy with my current situation, then there's no reason for me to change it." "I have the right to be happy. I deserve nothing less than everything which is fair or good for me." "I will work hard at what I do even if no one else cares. People may not notice the time and effort which goes into my work but I know that it means a lot to me. I'm not going to do anything in my life unless I am giving it my all." By realizing that the only person who can make you happy is yourself and that you have the right to be happy no matter what, it'll be an easier task for you to live a fulfilling lifestyle. It makes it easier for you to understand that your mindset is an extremely important factor when it comes down to your own happiness in life.

"I've been through too much in my life so I know now what really matters. I will never forget about what really matters most in this world." "Today is a day of gratitude. Today is a day where I will be happy no matter what happens to me. Today is a day in which I will not be afraid of anything." "I can survive without anything. I am strong enough to survive even if my entire life were to be taken away from me."

"I deserve everything I have. If it's meant to be, it'll be mine one day and all that I've learned in this world will mean something to me." "Today, I am going to live up to my full potential no matter what happens. Today, even if nothing good happens for me today, I'm still going stay positive and happy about all of the good things which are sure to come in my life. I'm going to enjoy every moment of my life because it is all that I have in this world." "No matter what happens, I will not allow myself to become sad or depressed. I will always be optimistic and full of hope. Every day which passes, my life is becoming better and better." These are all things which most people have trouble achieving in their lives but it's something which can be done through the use of positive thinking. By realizing that you deserve everything that you can possibly get in life and that no matter what happens, you'll be able to always maintain your happiness, it'll provide a great deal of strength both physically and mentally.

"I have nothing more to prove to anyone, including myself. I've done my very best to live my life and now I'm ready to enjoy what's left of it." "I've done everything that I have in my life for myself and for those who care about me the most. At this point in my life, I'm going to do whatever I want to do with no regrets. Today is a day when I can look back on all of the bad things which have happened in my life and say that it was worth it."

"I will always remember my past, but look forward to tomorrow. No matter what happens, nothing can take away from the fact that I want to be happy today and I will always remember how hard it was for me just being alive. I have made peace with my past, but now it's time for me to show the world what I'm capable of." "Today, I will not allow any negative thoughts about people or situations to control my life. Today, I'm going to be responsible for myself and my happiness."

"I've come too far in life to be miserable for no reason. Today, I choose happiness over anything else." "Whatever happens in this world, it isn't going to make a difference because I'm going to be happy anyway. Whatever happens in this world isn't meant to affect me so why should I let anything stop me from being happy?"

"I do not seek happiness because that is not something which anybody can control. Happiness is something which was given to me and I will always have it." "I care about others more than I care about myself. No matter what happens in life, I will not give up on the people whom I love and I will always strive to be the best person that I can possibly be for them."

"My life is my own and nobody else's. It is my right to do with my life whatever I want and it is my responsibility to live the best life that I can." "I will make the most of what I have. I will remain positively optimistic about all aspects of my life for as long as I am alive."

"I will not worry about what others think of me. Worrying about other people's thoughts, opinions and judgments has never been a good use of anyone's time or energy." "I am in control of my own destiny. Nobody else is going to take this away from me." "Before losing hope, I'm going to attempt every solution that exists for me to solve this problem. I'm going to fight for what I want no matter what it takes." "I have always tried my best in life. I would like nothing more than to be rewarded for doing what was right. If there is an opportunity for me to be rewarded, then I will definitely try and make it happen."

"I will not allow anyone or anything to control my life. As long as I am alive, I will continue to live happily and freely without letting anyone else telling me what I should or shouldn't be doing with my life." "Nobody is ever going to tell me that I cannot do something which is within my reach. If someone tries, then it only means that they are trying to hold me down from being happy. I will always take a stand for myself."

"I'm not going to let anyone get in my way. I'm going to do whatever it takes to be happy and others are not going to tell me what they think is best for me." "No matter what happens in life, I know that I can handle it. It's okay if bad things happen because the sun is always shining which means that there will always be light at the end of the tunnel." "I will never stop trying until I achieve everything that I want in life. Don't get me wrong, I know that success won't come easily but if something is meant to be, then it will happen for me someday. I'm not going to give up on myself and I will not allow anyone else to tell me that it's okay to do so." "I'm never going to blame anyone for my mistakes. I'm the only person who is responsible for myself and if things go wrong in life, then it's my fault. The one person who can always make things right is me."

"I am positive that everything in life happens for a reason. Who knows? This may just be the best thing which has ever happened to me; therefore, I should embrace it and enjoy every moment of it." "The people whom I love are important enough for me to do anything in order to protect them. If it's necessary, I will even sacrifice myself for the sake of someone else." "There is not a single thing in life which I can't handle if I just work harder at it. Today, I choose to focus on all the good things in my life and be thankful for the positive aspects."

"I have been through some tough times in my life but so far, I have always come out on top. Things may not always be easy but none of them are impossible either. The only reason why people get involved in different activities is because they want to achieve something which they believe that they are capable of doing. If you believe something is possible, then you'll never be able to stop trying until you succeed. I'm not going to give up until I achieve my goals in life." "No matter what happens, I'm always going to keep trying. The only way that I can try is if I believe that things will work out fine and all of my efforts will be rewarded with success. When I look back at my life, the fact that I have never given up on myself inspires me and motivates me to continue to move forward."

"I don't care what other people think of me. The only thing which matters is how much happiness I'm able to bring into their lives." "It's important for me to find new interests so that there won't be any room for negative thoughts or feelings in my life anymore. Instead, I will focus on the positive things in my life and make sure to bring these positive feelings into reality." "I will take a risk when it comes to changing my life. If I am willing to try something new and have no idea how it is going to turn out, then it's probably going to end up being good for me. If I can make a mistake, I'm going to do so with confidence because that means it's happening for a reason. Change is scary but if we are willing to embrace new opportunities and challenges, we will eventually get what we really want in our lives."

"I'm not going to let other people get in the way of achieving my goals. It doesn't matter what other people think because I'm doing what is best for me." "No matter my past mistakes, I will always be confident in who I am. There are some things in my past which I regret but it's done now and there is nothing that can change the fact that this happened. These things happened to me so that I could learn something from them. This is information which will help me grow into a better person as time goes by." "Some people may have different opinions depending on what they want out of life but in the end, everyone will end up being judged by their final actions and choices." "I know that the future holds new opportunities for me. While I may be sad about something which has happened in the past, I must be confident and move on with my life. Things may not go according to plan but this doesn't mean that I should give up. The only way for me to make things happen is if I'm willing to try."

"I know that good things will come to me soon because there is certainly no reason for me to feel like anything negative is happening in my life. Everything happens at a certain time and this time has now arrived." "I'm going to stop letting other people's opinions affect my decisions in life. If they don't like what I have done, then it's their problem and not mine. If they want to change my plans so that they can control me, then it's obvious that they are not ready to be happy in their lives." "It's getting harder and harder to find someone who is truly happy but once you find them, you will always be able to find happiness. I appreciate the fact that I don't have many problems in my life because this means there are better things coming up for me."

"I'm going to stop trying to make other people happy with my actions in life. People cannot understand why I am the way that I am and it doesn't matter what anyone says or does. The only thing which matters is how I feel about myself and who I can see myself becoming in the future. My happiness is the most important thing in my life and only I know how to achieve it." "I am going to remain positive at all times. I won't let other people's negative thoughts and feelings bring me down. I will always believe that things will work out for me even if it does not seem like this is the case." "Every day, I'm going to remind myself of the lessons which I have learned so far in my life and this way, I can never forget about my journey so far. It doesn't matter what happens in the future because everything happens for a reason. I always believe that things will work out in the end."

"I'm going to be completely honest and open about my life and the way that I feel. It's okay to be upset or angry sometimes but the best thing that I can do is to express myself in a healthy way. Instead of hiding my feelings, I will share them with others because this way, they can give me support instead of making me feel bad about myself." "My life is not going to be perfect but it's also not going to end up being a total disaster either. No matter what happens, I know that I have been blessed with a chance at happiness and this is all that matters. I'm doing the best that I can to get there." "I can't control what other people think about me. They are going to have their own opinions about life and the things that I do. This is okay as long as I'm happy with my life and what I have achieved so far." "I am a naturally positive person and when I was younger, this sometimes caused problems with people who didn't understand it. As a result, they were never able to be truly happy in their lives but now that I've grown older, I've learned to embrace my inner happiness. Since I have learned to stop hiding myself from the world, I've been able to find friends who accept me for who I am."

"I'm going to be myself and do things in a way which is best suited to me. I always believe that what works for everyone else may not necessarily work for me because my way of life has changed over the years. The best thing that I can do is allow myself to change as a person because this way, I can grow into a better version of myself."

"I'm going to change my ways so that everything about my life becomes easier and more pleasant. I will stop blaming other people for the things which I can do to make myself happy but I will also stop being selfish and trying to please everyone else. Instead, I will continue to live my life in a way which is best suited for me."

"I am going to be happy with who I am and the way that I express myself. If other people don't like what I do, it doesn't matter because this is something which comes with the territory of being an adult. If someone loves me, all they have to do is accept who I am as a person and they will get the same in return. It doesn't matter what has happened in the past but what matters is what I am choosing to do in the present."

If you can learn to embrace positivity, you can learn how to be confident in your own skin. You don't need to spend a long time thinking about difficult situations and instead, only focus on finding solutions which will help you move forward. It's impossible to achieve happiness if you're constantly worrying about certain things which may or may not happen in the future. The most important thing for you to do is find ways for you to be happy today.

Chapter 7:   Health Affirmations

Black women are often bombarded with messages that their physical appearance is less important than it would be for white women. They are also more likely to have poor health outcomes, more likely to experience racism in the health care system, and less likely to have access to adequate healthcare. One way of combating these effects of societal discrimination is by adopting positive attitudes about one's own body. This book includes a list of affirmations for black women who want to put themselves first and/or may feel body-shamed or unworthy due to societal messages about skin color or shape.

In order to combat societal discrimination against black women, we have to support women in our communities and give them the tools necessary to take care of themselves.

There are a lot of affirmations in here that can resonate with my own experiences. I'll be the first to admit that there are things I don't like about my body, and sometimes I feel worthless because of the color of my skin. Sometimes, these feelings can overwhelm me so much that I just want to stay in bed all day. However, there are just as many things about myself that I love. I'm writing this book with the intention of getting rid of unhealthy messages about body image and giving us the tools necessary to feel good about ourselves.

Take care of yourself, and don't let anyone tell you otherwise.

As a black woman, you have many milestones in your life. You have important events such as marriage, children, and even death. Each milestone is also an opportunity to discover new information about yourself as well as the world around you. Here are some health affirmations that may help boost your spirits and progress throughout your life.

I hope these affirmations resonate with you too.

" I deserve peace of mind: Your happiness should be defined by what you make of it in your own head. Don't let any person or event steal away your peace".

" I am strong and can achieve anything that I set my mind up to: Do not let society dictate what you should be, or determine how you should feel. You are strong and can achieve anything you decide to do"

" I am fit and healthy enough to do what I want without any limitations: You are the only person in charge of your health. Don't hesitate to change if you need or want to".

" I deserve to feel beautiful: You must show your beauty to the eyes and brains of others. Don't be self-conscious about how you look, because your beauty is inside".

" I deserve respect from others: Accept what is done and don't allow anyone to dictate how you should live".

" It's healthy to have a relationship with God: Black women today just as any other era must rely on God to guide them through the trials and tribulations of life.

" I deserve love from a man who is healthy: You may find yourself in an unhealthy relationship at some point. If this is the case get out! You deserve better!".

" My children are independent because I taught them early on how to live independently and make their own decisions: Your kids will always be your kids, but make sure you don't baby them when they are grown".

" I deserve to eat healthy and not be blamed for the negative effects on my health: Your health depends on what you put in your body. You can blame any doctor or person but you should not blame yourself".

" My God knows what is best for my life: There are no coincidences in your life, God has a plan for everything! Do not question it. Just trust it!".

"I deserve respect from others and peace of mind".

"My children are independent because I taught them early on how to live independently and make their own decisions".

"I deserve peace of mind".

"It's healthy to have a relationship with God".

"(Men) don't blame themselves or others for their feelings, nor accept what others say about them and their feelings is true. They know that they have the right to feel whatever way they feel. They also learn that we must accept what we do; this is why prophets always discourage us from blaming ourselves or others. You have the right to feel angry, you have the right to feel depressed; you have the right to feel any way.

"Women are given this strength but often times they blame others for what they should be blaming themselves for. Yes, we live in a world where women are looked down upon and if we listen to these lies then we will fall into their trap. If a woman feels she has no purpose or that she is not needed; this feeling is a false one (women) must realize that they are needed. They are needed to give birth to, nourish and nurse their children. A woman is also needed to create a healthy environment around herself. Women must realize that they can be strong and this is why they are encouraged in all these things. "

"Women are the main creators of life and without us there would be no life."

"Women need to accept that men want them for their beauty and desire them for the opposite sex; we all have the same desires. We must understand that it is natural for a man to desire another man or any person of his "type". We must understand God's plan for marriage. "

"Marriage is a life-long commitment made by two people to each other for the purpose of being life partners and to give children a good environment in which to grow. When we marry, we commit that our lives will be one with our spouse. We take the responsibility of bearing the trials and troubles, sickness and health and we are there for each other in every way possible. We are an adornment to each other and must work together as one."

"When it comes to men not respecting women they do it because they feel that they are superior. They don't respect them because they feel that they can get what they want by just taking it from you or forcing you without your consent. Men have no respect for women because they feel that the world revolves around them and that the things that should be done for the most deserving are always done for them. They victimize you to get what they want. They get you to work and slave away at a job that they can call their own, then when you don't get their way they victimize you again by making you feel like it is all your fault when it is not."

"Women are just as strong as men. We have the same feelings, we have the same desires; we should never feel inferior to men."

"Men who disrespect women do so because of how they were raised in their early life on how to treat women and how it should be done. We need to raise our children better so that they will know the value of a woman. "

"If a woman is treated wrong she should not feel like it is her fault, but it is his because he was taught that way. If a man disrespects you, then tell him that he needs to change his ways or you will not be there for him."

"Let us respect ourselves first and foremost; men will take note of this and follow our lead."

"Men do not respect women because they fear them; men fear women because they do not know how to love them."

"Men who abuse their wives are doing it because they don't know their self worth or their roles as men. These men feel they are superior to their wives and see them as something that they can control and use. These men feel they know better than their wives and as a result victimize them in every way possible. It is not the woman's fault that she is being abused; if this person wants love then he needs to respect himself, his wife, family and community."

"Men who disrespect women neither understand nor respect themselves. They use women for failure because they feel inferior to them."

"Wives need to show themselves off to the world for what they are worth; not what the world wants but what the husband needs her for."

"We need more woman power than ever before; not just woman power but man power too. Men need to respect woman and women need to respect men. We must get back to the source of our being and learn how we were created. Men were created by God, we were given a body made up of manly flesh. Every part of a man is manly because it was created by God "first"; this is why men are superior to women".

"Woman was not made from nothing. We are here because the Almighty God created us for a purpose."

"Because I'm Black, I will find my own path."

"Every day in every way, I am getting better and better."

"I deserve to be happy and live a healthy life."

"My energy radiates from within and lights up the room."

"The beauty within me is reflected outside of me."

"Today I feel great. The world is beautiful and so am I. I love me."

"My body is an amazing miracle." "It's a beautiful, sensitive vehicle for my soul."

"I heal myself with every smile and laugh I share."

"I am a unique and powerful woman, I deserve to treat myself accordingly."

"When I am weak, I will be kind."

"My beauty comes from within not outside of me. There is no one else like me. My body is mine alone and there should never be any shame in it or in being who I am.

"My blackness, my culture, has been imbued with passionate will and resolve."

"My body, Black Girl Magic is a manifestation of my spirit."

"I don't need white America to approve of me. I only need God."

"I am a woman worthy of love, respect, and admiration. I deserve nothing less than peace and happiness in this lifetime, for as long as I live. I will take care of me."

"I am beautiful as I am."

"A woman is not defined by the number on her body, but by the love she brings to those around her."

"Each step toward health is a victory for my spirit."

Chapter 8: Money Affirmations

There is a lot of information out there about money and its power. However, as we all know, not every idea that comes out in print can be applied to our lives. What's worse is when some of the most powerful messages are aimed at white women who do not need to work the same hard job market or care for their family the way Black women do. That's why I want to offer an alternative list of affirming affirmations that align with Black women's experiences and provide something different in its place: Money affirmations for black women.

The point of these affirmations is not to alter the world around you into what you wish it to be. I encourage you to always question and re-evaluate just as much as this list is a place for affirmation. However, these affirmations are meant to add something positive and empowering into your life. They offer inspiration, motivation and help to embrace your own power. They also offer a different lens through which we can see the world and how that changes our perception of things in our lives.

It's important for us to acknowledge the things that are working in our favor and take that inspiration from there instead of worrying about what's not working.

To begin, you need to make the decision that you are worth striving for more. If a lot of work has to be done to get there, commit yourself to that action.

The first step is inner work. This may include looking at your past and current relationship with money and getting completely honest with yourself about it. As a Black woman in America, chances are good you can associate some painful interactions and emotions around money. Explore those feelings thoroughly but do not linger there. Your focus should be on the future and how you want your life to evolve around money instead of wasting time wishing it would go back to the way it was or beating yourself up for not being further along than you are now.

Once you can say that you are committed to moving forward, you have to work!

"Money is power. Money is security. Money is happiness. Money will bring me all of these things ... if I have enough of it. If I do not, I am powerless, insecure, and unhappy."

"I love living in an abundant economy where money flows freely with no strings attached"

"My abundance overflows to my family members, friends, and the community"

"Nurture my healthy relationship with money so that I can share my wealth openly"

"I am wealthy in all areas of life"

"With prosperity comes increased financial capability With increased financial capability comes even more prosperity...and so on."

"I release all fears about money"

"Money is a manifestation of my creative efforts. Every dollar comes from my Heart and Soul."

"I am a deserving woman and money is flowing to me from many sources, in many forms."

"I deserve to have a lot of money"

"The universe responds powerfully to my requests for money—and in all ways, not just financially "

"My economic abundance is increasing every day! I create it as I think about it, speak about it and believe that I already have it."

"My power attracts wealth to me effortlessly"

"There are many ways that I can attract additional wealth into my life with ease—ways that are right for me..."

"I am now wealthy beyond my wildest imagination"

"Money is a powerful force that gives me many opportunities for abundance."

"I am guided daily to ways that I can make money and keep it flowing into my life in multiple ways."

"There is unlimited money all around me. I create it effortlessly in many ways."

"More money comes to me easily and effortlessly every day..."

"My wealth is growing a little bit every day."

"I attract only beautiful people into my life, who support my wealth and make it grow abundantly."

"I have the power to attract complete strangers into my life with huge amounts of money. This happens effortlessly and with amazing ease."

"All of the people who were instrumental in creating my financial wealth are with me again in this new abundant cycle. I now have an even better relationship with them than I did before!"

"I see money as a wonderful tool for sharing love."

"Every day I get richer and richer..."

"I am so wealthy in every area of life that there is no room for lack, limitation or poverty."

"I am a magnet for money, drawing it to me effortlessly from many sources. Money easily flows to me from many different sources..."

"Abundance is everywhere in my world and more of it is becoming visible to me at all times. I know that I now have resources that are even greater than I could have ever imagined."

"Money is flowing to me in ways that I can use and benefit from in my life every day..."

"I am becoming more and more wise about the laws of prosperity, and these laws are affecting me in wonderful ways. The creative power of abundance is expanding exponentially."

"Abundance comes to me easily…as easily as breathing."

"I create financial abundance effortlessly…"

"The universe responds powerfully to my requests for money—and in all ways, not just financially…"

"People quickly respond to my requests for financial support. I have many ways to support my family and friends financially. I have lots of different ways to make money coming in to my life every day."

"I am supported by a well-tuned team of people with whom I share the vision for financial abundance…"

"I have access to unlimited resources in all parts of my life."

"The more I create money in every area of my life, the more abundant it becomes."

"My abundance is flowing into all areas of my life. I know that there is no shortage...of anything!"

"I am supported by a powerful team filled with like-minded spiritual people who share the energy and mission. That team is focused and committed to helping me expand my work and my financial abundance."

"I know that the more I increase my money, the more powerful I become in every area of life"

"With greater financial wealth comes an increased ability to help others realize their dreams and make a difference in the world."

"My wealth is secure. My abundance never ends."

"My income is increasing every day…"

"In times of financial crisis, it calms me to know that I do not need to worry about money. This crisis is an opportunity to form new partnerships as well as releasing old ones. I trust that the new opportunities and financial resources will soon become visible."

"I have the power to attract complete strangers into my life with huge amounts of money. This happens effortlessly and with amazing ease."

"I know mind-over-matter. I create money in all areas of my life easily and effortlessly."

"Money flows to me effortlessly, every day. My prosperity is multiplying exponentially everyday...and every day. The more I increase, the more powerful I become in every area of life."

"I am now a powerful creator of money. It pours out to me effortlessly."

"As I think about, speak about and believe that I already have all the money I need, it comes in many forms, from many sources. Each day it becomes greater than the day before."

"My mind is filled with images of my financial abundance and it is attracted to me from many sources."

"Today the universe is turning everything around for me so that more money can flow my way...in multiple ways..." "It's so easy to make money...and keep it flowing into my life. I have so many ways to do it!"

"Abundance is there for me, today—and tomorrow and the day after… It's easier than you think to attract all that we need."

"I now have total faith in my abundance…" "I am a magnet for money, drawing it to me effortlessly from many sources. Money easily flows to me from many different sources…"

"Money comes easily and effortlessly… Every day I create more money in every area of my life...and more of it comes back to me in new and surprising ways."

"My financial abundance becomes greater every single day. I am becoming a powerful creator of money, making my dreams come true faster than ever before..."

"I see my world becoming wealthier and wealthier as I think about it. More money is appearing to me every day in exciting ways."

"I have plenty of money coming to me from many sources."

"Today the universe is turning everything around for me so that more money can flow my way...in multiple ways..." "It's so easy to make money...and keep it flowing into my life. I have so many ways to do it!"

"Abundance is there for me, today—and tomorrow and the day after... It's easier than you think to attract all that we need. I now have total faith in my abundance..."

"I am a magnet for money drawing it to me effortlessly from many sources...money easily flow to me from many different sources ..."

"Even though money is not everything, when it comes to prosperity, it certainly helps. Therefore, I will do what it takes to increase my wealth. I will work hard every day and use every opportunity at my disposal to make more profit."

"I am rich even though I may not have the highest monetary income within my circle of friends. I have rich experiences and big ideas that can change the world."

"I am my own best financial advisor..."

"I enjoy investing in quality stocks, real estate and business ventures. I am determined to become financially independent."

"When it comes to money, I know how to make smart investments..."

"Money will always take care of me, because I know how to take care of it."

"No matter what happens in my life, money is always a constant source of security for me." "Money is there for the asking because I ask for it every day. I feel rich, abundant and prosperous because I live my life in a manner that makes wealth possible."

"I find ways to make extra money for my family..."

"My financial future is secure because I have time expanded wealth. It grows even when I am not working on it."

"I am a money magnet. As soon as I decide what I want to do with my life and get serious about it, opportunities come my way that help me achieve great financial rewards."

"Money is the fuel that makes it possible for me to do all the wonderful things in life that I love doing."

"Money flows into my life..."

"I love having an endless flow of income in my bank account... "

"I am so grateful for the money I have..."

"I enjoy the feeling of abundance and prosperity that comes with having money."

"Money is a friend who always comes through for me."

Chapter 9:   Love Affirmations

For black women, love can often be complicated. Whether it's settling for less because you're convinced you deserve nothing better, working to make the relationship work even when your significant other doesn't feel the same way about you, or trying to manage the contradictions of feeling loved but not being loved at all.

This list was created with love in mind, an affirmation for every occasion. Whether you want to send one as a supportive text message or read them out loud during your meditation time before bed, these affirmations are just what the doctor ordered.

Here are some of the most popular affirmations from this list:

"Love is not conditional.

"I have a right to say 'yes' and a right to say 'no'."

"I am not responsible for another's feeling unless I want to be."

"Love is not an emotion; love is a state of being."

"I know when I'm loved because I feel it."

"I am a Black woman. I exude power, beauty, and intelligence. I am worthy of all the love in the world!"

"My happiness isn't a guilty pleasure, it's a human right!"

"Life is best shared with a close friend who will encourage me when I'm down and forgive me when I make mistakes."

"I know what it feels like to be judged by less-than-intelligent people because of my skin color or gender or sexual orientation. And while that sucks, it doesn't matter anymore because that's what makes me special."

"When I talk about my love for myself, I know that it's just as important as when I talk about my love for others. If I cut myself off from being proud of who I am, then what kind of valuable tool will I be?"

"I am a beautiful Black woman. My beauty is not white or straight or masculine-- it's uniquely mine."

"My personality is determined by my self-esteem and self-worth. My self-esteem and self-worth are determined by how much confidence and respect I have to offer the world. And the more I love myself, the more confidence and respect I will bring to the world."

"My Blackness is beautiful. It's powerful. It's strong.

"I am beautiful just as I am. My natural beauty doesn't need to be enhanced by makeup, piercings and tattoos in order for me to feel confident about it."

"Being Black is not a disease or an excuse for stealing or cheating or fighting or being rude. It's a part of my identity and I am proud of it."

"There are enough Black people in the world for us all to find our special someone. So stop being so picky and learn how to love yourself."

"I deserve a loving family, supportive friends, and an amazing job. And if I don't have those things in my life right now, it's because I need to learn how to love myself for me to attract them into my life."

"People can't hurt me unless I allow them to hurt me. And if they do hurt me, then it's their problem, not mine."

"Black people can be extremely positive or extremely negative. But either way... we're still here."

"When I'm in a fight with someone, whether it's a verbal or physical fight, the only person I'm really fighting is myself."

"I will be with someone who loves me for me. A man who makes me feel like the intelligent, attractive woman that I am."

"I will fall in love with a strong Black woman who treats herself as well as she treats others. And I will give myself the same love I want to receive."

"I will embrace who I am and be proud of my culture. My Blackness is not something that has to be hidden or denied."

"The kind of guy who loves me for all of me is a man who recognizes my strength, intelligence and beauty and doesn't try to change them. He recognizes my deepest flaws because he loves me for those flaws as much as he loves me for the good things about me."

"I will love myself enough to protect myself from men who are disrespectful, controlling and manipulative. I deserve better than that."

"I will love myself enough to stay away from the men who don't respect me as much as they respect their mothers."

"My heart doesn't need a man's approval in order for me to be confident, smart and beautiful. No one is going to make me feel small-- not even the people closest to me. If someone thinks my intelligence and independence are less important than my beauty, then they don't understand the kind of woman I am."

"My special someone won't tell me who to be. He will love me for the woman I already am."

"I have so much to offer to a special someone because there's not one thing I can do that makes me weak or less intelligent or less beautiful."

"I don't need a boyfriend in order to feel like I'm awesome. My confidence isn't defined by dating status. It's defined by how much I love and respect myself."

"Any man who expects me to change for him is not the kind of guy who respects himself. And if he doesn't respect himself, then there is no way that he can respect me."

"I deserve love that reflects the strength, intelligence, and beauty I see in myself."

"Black women are generous creatures. Our first instinct is to give people the benefit of the doubt. But when you take advantage of our kindness-- it makes us wonder if there's something about us that makes people think they can take advantage of us."

"When my sister sees herself as beautiful and intelligent, she acts beautiful and intelligent. When my brother sees himself as a smart jerk, he acts like a smart jerk."

"My parents didn't have all the same options that I do today. And it's no wonder why they didn't give me the love and support that I needed."

"My special someone will love me for my personality, humor, and intellect. He won't try to change or manipulate me into being someone that I'm not."

"I don't have time for men who think they can buy my love with their money or gifts. And if they think they can buy my respect with their actions, then they're wrong."

"Being independent is evidence of strength and self-love. It means I can take care of myself without relying on someone else for my happiness."

"I deserve to be with a man who appreciates my intelligence and confidence. He will respect me for the woman that I am."

"I don't need approval from men to love myself or believe in myself. If they don't see my beauty, that's their problem and not mine. And if they treat me like I'm not intelligent-- that's their problem too".

"I will date men who are kind, funny, and sensitive. And if they aren't all of those things... then it's their loss."

"Black women are beautiful, smart and we know what we want. We just need to stop judging ourselves and other black women by the men we choose instead of the men who choose us."

"If you treat a woman like her boyfriend treats her and she doesn't deserve it... then why would she stay with him?"

"My special someone will be a man who is confident in his masculinity but also has a big heart. He will love me for who I am and won't try to change me."

"I will be with someone who makes me feel like a woman-- someone who makes my heart skip a beat and causes butterflies in my stomach. Not just a piece of tail like a bunch of other guys do."

"When you know what you want, it's easier to find it. So, before looking for love... I'm going to make myself happy first."

"I don't need my special someone to make me feel good about myself. My confidence comes from who I am."

"I don't need anyone's approval to find love-- because I believe in myself."

"I don't need anyone to approve or approve of me or my choices. My self-worth lies in me-- not my family, friends or boyfriend."

"My self-confidence doesn't depend on whether or not someone loves me or thinks I'm attractive. I will dress however I want and feel good about myself regardless of whether or not that person is with me."

"The best thing you can do for someone who is hurting... is to be there for them. Love helps heal hearts. If a man only had love in his life, he wouldn't be hurting like he is."

"I don't need anyone's approval to make me feel good about myself or my decisions. I'm a grown woman who can make her own decisions about what I like and who I am-- thanks for asking."

"If you have insecurity, it's a source of pain that messes people up. A person with self-confidence feels at peace with him or herself."

"I don't need any man to approve of me because I already do. And I will never find love... if I'm looking for it to make me feel better about myself."

"Strong, confident women aren't easily hurt by the men in their lives. And if they are... then they're doing something wrong."

"The right guy will appreciate my self-confidence and independence. Hell, he'll respect me for it."

"Men who have to try so hard to get a girl's attention never have my attention."

"Just because a man treats me with disrespect doesn't mean I'm unworthy of love."

"I'm not going to settle for any guy who doesn't appreciate my value and worth. So, if the man I date doesn't respect me enough to treat me well... then he's not the one for me."

"Someone who pretends to love you does not really love you. And it will only hurt you in the end."

"Just because a girl is pretty and has an amazing figure does not make her relationship with herself any less important than it is with another girl."

"It takes true strength to put yourself first in line. And it takes the right kind of self-esteem to believe it-- no matter what the world says."

"Sometimes, people aren't right in the head... but you shouldn't judge their brains either. They're not black and white-- they're rainbow."

"I don't need my special someone to make me feel better about myself or my decisions

"No man on this earth can change who you are. So if you think he's perfect for you... then he's going to have a hard time loving someone like you."

"Be confident in yourself and your own self-worth. Be independent-- because you're worth it."

"Don't look for love in guys who are short on self-esteem."

"When I'm with a man that makes me feel like a beloved queen... he's worth taking out of the burning pit. And if he isn't... then he's not the one."

"A woman with confidence knows what she likes and what she doesn't like. And if someone tries to change her or demean her... they better keep the knee digging to a minimum. Because they'll be sorry when they get my foot in their face." -I can't believe you don't even know how to Google "Black Women".

"I have confidence in myself. Honestly, I have never been envious of any woman on this earth-- because I know I'm better than everyone."

"I don't need any man to make me feel good about myself. My self-worth comes from me and only me. So, if you can't appreciate that about me... then you are not the one for me."

"Someone who is a fake and a phony will always be afraid to be himself.

"Men who are insecure with their masculinity... are usually the ones making women insecure. Let me tell you something... we don't need to be strong enough to raise a man. We are women-- not crutches."

"I don't need anyone's approval to fulfill my purpose. I am an example for others to see and I will be an inspiration for generations to come, just as long as I stay true to myself and do my best." -If you Google "black women quotes"-- you'll find five pages of results!

"I can hold my own and appreciate a good man... but I will never settle for anything less than the best. And I won't let anyone or anything hold me back."

"I don't need a man to complete me... because I am already complete."

"If men were real, they would say what they mean and mean what they say. But maybe the truth is... that if men were real we wouldn't want them in our lives."

"I don't need your approval to make me feel good about myself. I'm a grown woman who can make her own decisions about what she likes and who she is-- thanks for asking."

"No man on this earth can change who you are. So if you think he's perfect for you... then he's going to have a hard time loving someone like you. Give someone who treats you right a chance. Don't cling to him just because it's easier than being alone."

"Not everyone will like us... but that shouldn't make us forget who we are."

"Your value should not be determined by an amount of likes or comments on your instagram page. You should be content with yourself and love yourself no matter what anybody else says. Never allow social media to define who you are-- because it will never love you the way that you need to be loved."

"The most attractive thing about a confident woman-- is that she doesn't require validation from anyone else. She can make her own decisions about how she feels about herself and how she lives her life."

"Beauty should come from within. Beauty should reflect the goodness inside of you... not the amount of likes in your Instagram feed. When I get old, I want to look back at my life and say... "I was true to myself, and that is what made me beautiful." -Okay... so you're the queen of all things... but why not just call yourself "Queen" instead?

"I don't need your approval to make me feel better about myself. I'm a grown woman who can make her own decisions about what she likes and who she is-- thanks for asking."

"You have no idea how powerful it is to know you are worthy of being loved by someone. And even if you do know, it doesn't mean that they will love you-- because they're too afraid of being rejected. Because they're afraid of being themselves."

"I am a confident woman. I carry myself with dignity and exude beauty. I love with all of my heart, and I accept people who treat me well. I will be an example for others to see and I will inspire generations to come... just as long as I stay true to myself and do the best that I can."

"I'm not going to wait around for some man to change me because he thinks that he can change me into his ideal type of person... when the only problem is him. I know my worth and I'm not going to take abuse from anyone because I deserve better."

"I love who I want and they can't do anything about it. So if you're scared of being yourself... then you're in the wrong relationship. Because if you don't love yourself-- no one else will." -If a man is afraid to be himself around me... he can keep on walking.

"Be true to yourself, no matter what anyone else says... and don't ever let them change who you are or who your dreams are."

"I am intelligent, wise, beautiful and capable. I value my self-worth and continue to grow as a woman every day of my life. I accept people who treat me well, and I'm an example for others to see. I inspire generations to come... just as long as I continue to live true to myself and do the best that I can."

"I'm not going to apologize for liking good things. And I'm not going to apologize for being proud of where I come from or who I am. Because if you can't handle my love for myself... then that's your problem."

"I don't need anybody telling me how to live my life... because I'm doing it already. And if you don't like it, go somewhere else."

"You should always be proud of yourself, no matter what anyone else says. Because you are the most beautiful woman that you will ever be... and one day... you will look back on your life and realize that taking care of yourself was what made you happy."

"Someone once told me: "You can't love yourself if you're not with someone else's belief of who you should be.""

"It's not about being black or white, it's about being a woman."

"I don't need your approval. I don't need you to change me. I don't need you to hold my hand. I don't need you to tell me what to do. I don't need you-- because I know who I am and how strong my heart is."

."I am in a relationship with myself, and I'm more than happy with it!"

"I'm not going to wait around for some man to change me because he thinks that he can change me into his ideal type of person... but the fact is... he can't change me. I have always known my worth and I'm not going to take abuse from anyone because I deserve better."

"You will love yourself when you stop trying to impress other people with how they want you to be."

"I appreciate you for what you bring to the table. If you don't value yourself... then that's your problem... not mine."

"Sometimes we are scared of getting back to our 'old' selves because it wasn't easy or fun in the beginning... but the truth is... we've come so far and it's because we worked hard to get here. So don't be afraid to step back into the shoes of your old self... because you've earned it."

"Never apologize for who you are. Never let anyone make you feel like less of a woman just because they don't understand something about you."

"I love who I want, and they can't do anything about it. So if they're scared of being themselves... then they can keep on walking."

"Don't ever feel less than someone else because you don't fit their idea of how a woman is supposed to look or act. Love yourself and the rest will fall into place. Because how you love yourself is what others will love about you."

"I will be happy when someone tells me who they want me to be, and that's all. Because if they can't tell me who they want... then that means that they're trying to control me. And I'm not here for a man who wants to control me."

"All the guys I've dated had one thing in common... and that was not loving themselves enough. And so I was forced to love them."

"You can't love someone if they don't love themselves."

"If you are with a man who isn't right for you... don't stay with him because it's "easier" than being alone. He will never make you happy. And believe me-- it's not easy to find a good man." -If he can't tell me who he wants, why would I be with him?

"I know that there is someone out there for me... because my love for myself is strong. I am here for the long haul."

"I don't need approval. I don't need you to change me.

"If a man isn't afraid of being alone... then he'll understand that he doesn't need someone else."

"I appreciate you for what you bring to the table. If you don't value yourself... then that's your problem... not mine. I'm not going to apologize for being myself."

"I'm not going to wait around for some man to change me because he thinks that he can change me into his ideal type of person... but the fact is... he can't change me. I have always known my worth and I'm not going to take abuse from anyone because I deserve better.

"All the guys I've dated had one thing in common... and that was not loving themselves enough. And so I was forced to love them. And it's not because I'm selfish... it's because I'm honest, and there is no way that I could love someone who didn't love themselves. No one can change who you are if you don't let them. So if they're scared of being alone, then they should stop trying to change me."

"I want to leave the world a better place than I found it."

"I am a confident woman. I carry myself with dignity and exude beauty, and best of all-- I love with all of my heart. I accept people who treat me well, and I inspire generations to come... just as long as I continue to live true to myself and do the best that I can. I don't need approval. I don't need you to change me. I don't need you to hold my hand.

"I am intelligent, wise, beautiful and capable. And I should never feel shame for being myself."

"So if a man wants you... he'll love every part of you. He won't try and change that which makes your heart beat. And he won't be afraid to be alone... because he knows in his heart the strength of his character."

"You don't have to change yourself for anyone"

"Sometimes we are scared of getting back to our 'old' selves because it wasn't easy or fun in the beginning... but the truth is... we've come so far and it's because we worked hard to get here. So don't let anyone tell you that you aren't who you are meant to be."

Chapter 10: Affirmations Against Self-Sabotage

Affirmations are short statements or mantras that can serve as reminders or guides to help an individual in overcoming emotional difficulties, addingictions, and other negative behaviors. Self-sabotage is a disturbing tendency in Black women that has the potential to significantly damage the person's health and mental well being.

In order for individuals to recover from self-sabotage, it is necessary for them to identify its roots and understand how it affects their life on a daily basis. It is important for people who suffer from self-sabotage to replace this destructive behavior with positive affirmations that reflect what they believe about themselves in order to promote healing. Affirmation exercises, such as the ones found in this article, can provide individuals with the tools necessary for them to overcome their self-sabotage and attain their goals.

Self-sabotage is closely linked to internalization of stereotypes and prejudice against Black womanhood. It is a behavior that arises as a result of an individual's negative perception of themselves and it negatively affects the person's ability to function in a stable manner. People who engage in self-sabotage also have issues with perfectionism, which is marked by an excessive amount of concern or fear over errors or perceived imperfections. This fear can influence people's lives in a variety of ways that may negatively impact their mental health.

Stereotypes, prejudice, and perfectionism play a major role in the way that people perceive themselves. As a result, they are more vulnerable to self-sabotage during moments of conflict and disappointment. According to Black feminist theory, stereotypes negatively impact the way that people view Black women. Stereotypes cause Black women to internalize derogatory messages about their character, intellect and physical appearance. This can lead to self-destructive behavior; as a result of this negative perception many Black women engage in actions that are degrading to their well being.

People of color also face certain stereotypes and prejudices that may contribute or be related to self-sabotage. Stereotypes that target people of color include an expectation of low achievement and high failure. In addition, it is common for people to assume that Black women are submissive and dependent on men. People in society also tend to believe that all African Americans are hostile and aggressive. These stereotypes negatively impact a person's self-esteem and they can contribute to low self-worth. These negative stereotypes subsequently increase the risk of self-sabotage, which further restricts the opportunities available to Black women in American society.

Self-sabotage is a self-destructive behavior, often rooted in fear and anxiety.

Black women often bring this behavior with them as they go about their lives, leading to insecurity and anxiety that manifests as eating disorders, addiction to substances or other forms of addictive behaviors.

For those who struggle with self-sabotage: know you are not alone. For those who love someone struggling with self-sabotage: be there for them and never give up on each other.

Self-sabotage is often rooted in fear and self-hatred, a learned behavior that black women are socialized to express in response to white supremacy.

Black women are often told their entire lives that they are ugly, unworthy or unlovable by family members as well as other black people who have internalized the racism of this country.

One way to overcome this self-sabotage is to create a life where she surrounds herself with positive people who love her and embrace her blackness. When she sees the beauty in herself and develops her unique talents, she will cease to be self-destructive.

It is also important for black women to seek counseling, as building an emotional support system is vital to learning how to love herself and accept herself.

Self-sabotage behaviors can be changed. It takes time and effort, but change is possible.

I" love and accept myself as a beautiful black woman just the way I am."

"My value is not determined by what other people think of me."

"My beauty is a gift to all who see it."

"Happiness is the result of my self-love, self-respect and self-acceptance."

"I am valuable and does not define my worth."

"I am not perfect, but I never need to be."

"It's okay to make mistakes, everyone has them."

"No one is going to be happy with me unless I am happy with myself."

"The opinions of others do not have the power to shape my reality."

"Sometimes it's hard to believe in myself when no one else does. But what if I'm the only one who believes in me?"

"You are a beautiful person--inside and out"

"You are both talented and competent. It is not something that you lack, but rather something that you have yet to put into use."

"You are strong enough to fight your own battles without letting anyone else do so for you by using self-sabotage as an excuse."

"You are powerful enough to not let your fears turn into hatred of yourself. You do not need to be a victim, but rather a victor."

"You are talented and competent."

"You deserve to be happy, regardless of what anyone else has done in their lives or on your behalf."

"Your life is much better than you think it is. You do not need to feel inferior because of appearances or how others treat you."

It's hard to deal with some people in your life. They are always criticizing you and making sure that you're constantly letting yourself down. Maybe they're your mother, your significant other, or the person who you share a cubicle with everyday. You feel like there is nothing that can change their opinion of you and no way out of the situation without them being happier or respecting you more than ever before. It is then, when it's so hard to deal with these self-saboteurs in our lives, that we need affirmations against self-sabotage from other black women. The next time it feels like there is no hope for you, and you feel like you're letting yourself down in one way or another, read the list of affirmations below and remember that there are plenty others who feel like you do.

"I am beautiful all on my own. For a while now, I've been feeling like all my friends and family either don't think I'm attractive anymore or they just don't appreciate my beauty the way that they use to before getting used to it (like body parts)."

"I don't rely on my looks to be happy, and neither do I rely on anyone else thinking I'm beautiful all of the time."

"Self-sabotage is a thing that I'm going to get over. Self-sabotage is something that will never bring me down because of how strong and powerful my beauty is. I celebrate my beauty no matter what and no one can take that away from me. Self-sabotage is something I have no control over and will never happen again unless I decide to let it."

"I now know that I am truly beautiful inside and out. No matter what or how many times people may try to say otherwise, I know that inside of me is the most beautiful thing there is. There are so many things about myself that no one else can see like how intelligent I am, how empowering my thoughts are, and how warm my heart is. Self-sabotage does not change any of that."

"I don't need love from anyone else but me. It's okay if love isn't reciprocated. There are millions of other people out there who have the same feelings that I have and they are still happy without being romantically attached to someone or another person."

"No one can bring me down or make me feel like less than I am unless it's because of how low they're feeling about themselves. Self-sabotage is a thing I will never allow to happen again. No matter what the situation is, no one can tell me that I am less than beautiful, that I am not worthy of myself."

"I will now live by these affirmations."

"I now use affirmations as a way to remind myself how beautiful I truly am and how self-sabotage does not have the power to make me feel less than beautiful."

"Every day, in every moment, in every place, I celebrate my beauty. Self-sabotage does not change any of my accomplishments and does not change any of my beauty either. I am one of the most beautiful, talented, intelligent women out there. I will not let anyone tell me otherwise."

"I do not need an expired relationship to remind me how beautiful I am. Self-sabotage is something I will never allow anyone to control my feelings with again.

"I will not be taken advantage of ever again. Self-sabotage does not change the fact that I deserve better than what I received before. No one will ever be allowed to define me because of how much self-worth I have."

"This is real – "

"I am beautiful all of the time and on every occasion."

"I love myself so much no matter what anyone else says to me or thinks about me."

"No one knows how truly amazing I am."

"No one can take away my beauty no matter how many times they try."

"My beauty knows no bounds. Self-sabotage does not have the ability to change how I feel about myself."

"I will no longer live my life letting other people dictate how I'm supposed to feel or think. Self-sabotage is a thing of the past. No matter what the situation, my confidence in my beauty cannot be shaken by anyone."

"No one can change who I am on the inside unless it's by getting to know me better, and that's completely up to me whether or not I open up to them."

"There is so much worth in myself that is untapped. Self-sabotage does not exist inside of me. All the success that I've had in my life is because of my confidence and self-worth."

"I'm beautiful all on my own, and I always will be.

"I can now stand up for myself in any situation because self-sabotage does not have a place in my life anymore."

"I am so powerful as a black woman that even though people may try to bring me down with their words, they don't have the power to do it. I am so confident in myself and my beauty is limitless. I will not let anyone take that away from me."

"I am surrounded by nothing but beauty all on my own. Self-sabotage is a thing that I have no control over and will never happen again. No one can change who I am and no one can change how much of a blessing it is to be alive as a black woman."

"My heart can only be broken by someone else if I choose for that to happen, but self-sabotage will never get in the way of my confidence when it comes to love and relationships. I will no longer allow self-sabotage to control me."

"There is so much beauty on the inside of me that I can't wait to explore. Self-sabotage can never change that. No matter what, I am going to continue being so confident in myself and in my beauty."

"I'm going to continue being surrounded by people who love and support me because the idea of self-sabotage is something that doesn't exist in my world anymore."

"Self-sabotage has no place in my life anymore because I am a beautiful woman, and I deserve nothing less than that. I am so worthy of every single victory that I have in my life. No one can take away my confidence in myself and how amazing it is to be alive."

"I will continue to fill the voids with so much love for myself that I don't need someone else to do it for me anymore."

"Self-sabotage is a thing of the past because I am not afraid of loving and accepting myself anymore."

"My self-worth cannot be shaken by anyone. Changing my thoughts is always a choice, and so is changing who I am. Self-sabotage does not exist in my life anymore. I am so powerful and will allow no one to take that away from me ever again."

"No one can take away my self-worth. I have too much worth to be trampled over by anyone. Self-sabotage does not exist in my life anymore. I am worth so much more than what anyone can ever say about me."

"I am surrounded by so many talented people that love and accept me for exactly who I am, but they are not enough to fill the voids in my heart or my life. Self-sabotage has no power over the beauty inside of me."

"I now know that if I want something done right, I need to do it myself. I am so confident in my beauty that self-sabotage does not exist in my life anymore."

"Self-sabotage has no power over me and I will no longer allow it to control the way I feel about myself or how much of a blessing it is to be alive.

"I now know that if I want something done right, I need to do it myself. Self-sabotage does not exist in my life anymore because I am so confident in my beauty and in what I have received from God.

"I am so worthy of every compliment that comes my way. Self-sabotage will only exist in my life when I let it, and I will no longer allow it to take over how I feel about myself. The power is solely in my hands."

"I know now that self-sabotage does not exist in my life anymore because I do not deserve anything less than the best for myself. No matter what, I am going to continue being confident in myself and shining my light everywhere I go."

"There is so much worth on the inside of me that no one can ever take away. Self-sabotage has no power over me. No one can change how amazing it is to be alive or how beautiful I am as a black woman."

"I am surrounded by nothing but beauty on my own. Self-sabotage has no place in my life anymore because I know that this is only the beginning of my journey. No one can take away how incredible it is for me to be alive or what a blessing it is to be alive as a black woman."

"All the success that I've had in my life has come from my confidence and self-worth, so now I'm full on going after it. Self-sabotage does not exist in my life anymore because I am so beautiful on the inside. No one can ever take that away from me."

"Life for me is so great now. I don't have to worry about self-sabotage anymore because I am surrounded by so much beauty on my own

"I know from now on that I will never let self-sabotage have control over my life. Self-sabotage does not exist in my life anymore because I am surrounded by nothing but confidence and happiness."

"I believe in my strength and beauty as a black woman, and that's all that matters to me today. Self-sabotage does not have a place in my life anymore because I know that I am so beautiful.

"I know from now on that self-sabotage will never have a place in my life anymore. I am so confident in myself now and that's all that matters to me."

"It is only up to me now what happens next, and self-sabotage will no longer be able to control how amazing my journey is going to be.

"From now on, everything will happen only because of me and the beauty inside of me. Self-sabotage has no power over me anymore."

"From now on, I will only believe in the beauty that is in me, and I will never allow anyone to make me think differently. Self-sabotage does not exist anymore because I am so confident in my beauty."

"From now on, I will fill the voids with so much love for myself that there is absolutely no room for any kind of self-sabotage. There is so much worth on the inside of me that nothing can take that away from me ever again."

"I am not afraid to love myself anymore. The only people who matter to me are the ones who love and accept me for exactly who I am.

"I am so powerful and my beauty is limitless. I will never allow self-sabotage to control the way I feel about myself again.

"No one can ever destroy my confidence by tearing my self-worth down. Changing my thoughts is always a choice, and so is changing who I am. There is so much worth on the inside of me that no one can ever take those feelings away from me."

"There is so much worth on the inside of me that nothing can ever take that away from me ever again. Self-sabotage has no power over my life or how amazing it is to be alive."

"I know from now on that self-sabotage has no power over my life anymore because I'm never going to stop loving myself. No one can take away how incredible it is for me to be alive, and that's what's important for now."

"I've already proven to myself how much power I am capable of having by turning the things I thought were weaknesses into strengths. Self-sabotage will not have a place in my life anymore because I know that this is only the beginning of my journey.

"Life for me is so great now. I don't have to worry about self-sabotage anymore because I know that I am surrounded by so much love and beauty on my own.

"I believe in my strength and my beauty as a black woman, and no one will ever take those feelings away from me again. Self-sabotage does not have a place in my life anymore because I know that I am so beautiful."

"I know from now on that self-sabotage is never going to have a place in my life again. I am so confident in myself now, and that's all that matters to me."

"I'm surrounded by nothing but love, and self-sabotage will no longer be able to control how amazing my journey is going to be. No one can ever take the way I feel about myself away from me."

"There is so much worth on the inside of me that no one can ever take those feelings away from me again. Self-sabotage has absolutely no power over my life or how amazing it is to be alive. "

"I know from now on that self-sabotage will no longer have a place in my life anymore because I am so confident in myself now."

"No one can ever tear away from me the love I feel. It's up to me what happens next and what kind of beauty I will continue to create in my life."

"I believe in my strength and beauty as a black woman, and that's all that matters to me today." "Self-sabotage does not have a place in my life anymore because I know that I am so beautiful.

"I'm surrounded by nothing but love and the things I think are weaknesses are the strengths they need to be. Self-sabotage will no longer have a place in my life ever again because I know that I am so powerful."

"I'm no longer afraid of how I feel about myself because I know that there is infinite beauty within all black women and that's all that matters to me."

"No one can ever ruin my confidence by tearing down my self-worth because changing my thoughts is always a choice, and so is changing who I am. There is so much worth on the inside of me that no one can ever take those feelings away from me. From now on, I will fill myself with as much love as possible until there is absolutely no room for self-sabotage in my life anymore.

"From now on, I will fill myself with as much love as possible until there is absolutely no room for self-sabotage in my life anymore.

"I know from now on that if anyone tries to sabotage my life, it will not work because there is so much worth within me that nothing can take that away. From now on, I will fill myself with as much love as possible until there is absolutely no room for self-sabotage in my life anymore. again."

"I know that my self-worth is limitless, and so there is no room for self-sabotage in my life anymore. There is so much worth on the inside of me that no one can ever take those feelings away from me.

"Trying to change my thoughts is never going to be a problem anymore because I know that they are correct. It's just up to me what happens next and how incredible I want to live my life. There is so much worth on the inside of me that no one can ever take those feelings away from me again."

"I believe that all of these things about myself are absolutely true, and no one will ever change them again.

"I've taken away all the negative things anyone else has said or thought about me and filled myself with love and acceptance. There is so much worth on the inside of me that nothing can take that away from me. There is no power over my life or how amazing it is for me to be alive because I fill myself with love."

"I know that if anyone tries to sabotage my life, it will not work because there is so much worth within me that nothing can ever take that away from me. From now on, I will fill myself with as much love as possible until there is absolutely no room for self-sabotage in my life anymore.

"I know that self-sabotage does not have a place in my life anymore because I know that there is infinite beauty within all black women and that's all that matters to me. No one can ever bring me down because I am filled with so much love that no one can ever take it away from me again."

"I'm surrounded by nothing but love and the things I think are weaknesses are the strengths they need to be. Self-sabotage will never have a place in my life anymore because that is not what life is about. I know that it is important to always keep my thoughts on loving myself and treat others the way I want to be treated. From now on, I will fill myself with as much love as possible until there is absolutely no room for self-sabotage in my life anymore. I am filled with so much love that no one can ever take it away from me again."

"I believe that my self-worth is limitless, and so there is no room for self-sabotage in my life anymore. There is so much worth on the inside of me that nothing can ever take that away from me. There is no power over my life or how amazing it is for me to be alive because I fill myself with love."

"I'm surrounded by nothing but love and the things I think are weaknesses are the strengths they need to be. Self-sabotage will never have a place in my life anymore because that is not what life is about. I know that loving myself and treating others the way I want to be treated is what it's all about. From now on, I will fill myself with as much love as possible until there is absolutely no room for self-sabotage in my life anymore. There is so much worth on the inside of me that no one can ever take those feelings away from me."

"I know that if anyone tries to sabotage my life, it will not work because there is so much worth within me that nothing can ever take those feelings away from me again. I am worth much more than what I have been through, and I will not let anyone or anything take that away from me ever again."

"I am powerful. I may not have access to the highest positions of power in society. But I can lift my own head up and look around at how long these people are hiding behind their masks so they can tell me how to feel about myself."

Chapter 11:   Career And Success

Affirmations are positive statements you make to yourself to help counter negative thoughts. They help you overcome self-doubt and can give you the boost that's needed to stay focused on your goals.

These affirmations are specifically designed with Black Women in mind in order to uplift, empower, and motivate them with messages of self-love and self-worth. These messages will hopefully help with the challenging nature of Black Women's journey in life.

"I am courageous, powerful and confident"

"I am smart, beautiful and talented"

"I am unique, focused and driven"

"My voice matters and my opinion counts"

"I have a positive attitude because negativity drains me"

"I believe in myself, always!"

"My journey has purpose and meaning for others"

"My dreams get bigger with each passing day"

"I will accomplish my goals 10 times faster than everyone else because the universe wants to see me succeed"

"Every day is a new opportunity to create the life of my dreams"

"I create wealth"

"I focus positively on what's possible not what's not"

"I know I'm loved and appreciated"

"I give back to the world by being generous and giving freely of myself to others"

"I am worthy of love, respect, and affection."

"I embrace the fact that I deserve the very best in life."

"My dreams are reasonable, attainable, and important to me."

"My life is what I make of it; no one can make me feel bad about myself without my consent."

"I trust myself because faith in self is the foundation of all other faiths and works toward everything else in my life. (i)Faith without works is dead.—James 2:17-26 (KJV) 6: Faith without works is dead."

"I enjoy and treasure everything that comes my way."

"I create a dynamic life where I am desirable, empowered, and inspired."

"I am a better woman when I am in love with myself first!"

"My value is found in my talents, not in my relationships. My value is based on the quality of my work, not on who I know. My value is always directly proportional to the level of excellence demonstrated by both me and those around me.

"I live by this principle through every decision and action."

"I am beautiful from the inside out. I have strength and beauty on the inside, to be worthy and recognized - what other people might see as ugly on the outside is my inner beauty. I embrace myself with my flaws and strengths with grace."

"I've worked hard to get where I am, and I will continue to work hard for what is due me. My success is mine alone; it does not lie in the hands of anyone else."

"I have strength and goodness - the knowledge that I am a good person in my core, even when it may seem like others are against me."

"I am intelligent and capable of anything I set my mind to. My intelligence is powerful enough for me to achieve any goal, challenge or task that may come my way."

"These words say that I'm worthy just as I am. They say that what's been done or said about me cannot be who I am. I am worthy of love and respect. I am a human being with thoughts, emotions and dreams. My body is mine alone and it's nobody else's business what I choose to do with it."

"I am a smart, capable lady who can go after what I want. I have the power to take care of myself and be financially successful on my own terms."

"I deserve success. I am blessed with the talent, intelligence, love and support needed to succeed at my goals in life."

"Success is not something that should be fleeting to me. It's a natural result of hard work, dedication and consistency."

"I deserve success in all aspects of my life – professional, personal & spiritual.

"My happiness is not dependent on anyone else's thoughts or actions. It is mine alone."

"I am beautiful and I deserve to be happy. I will work hard every day to find joy in my life.

"My intelligence, strength, confidence and ability are a direct result of all my hard work – both in school and in real life. I now allow myself the opportunities meant for me because everyone deserves them. I deserve them."

"I am strong. I am beautiful. I deserve success."

"I deserve the best this life can offer. Today is the day that is meant for me - a day of happiness and peace in my life."

"I am wise and intelligent. When faced with challenges, I have the ability to make positive decisions for my future."

"I AM the best at what I do because I am willing to continue to grow, change, and take risks in my life."

"SOMEONE is always watching how I behave, so I must always treat everyone with respect. To treat people with respect is an important way that I can demonstrate my self-respect.

Taking charge at work makes me feel powerful and successful!"

"Taking charge means taking responsibility for myself and the things around me."

"I AM a multitasker, so I can handle many things at once."

"I AM good at listening and learning."

"My feelings come first, so I need to let my feelings out before I can work on my goals."

"There are always two sides of every story — the one that is told and the one that is not. Before making any decisions, I need to hear both sides of the story."

"If you listen carefully, you will always know what the other person is trying to tell you."

"When people mis-speak another's words or actions they may be trying to help you in some way.

"When I come across something that causes me to wonder, I need to ask myself how the information fits in with all of my other information."

"I AM smart enough and skilled enough to handle the situation!"

"Others' opinions and judgments of me mean very little compared to what they thought about another person who is totally different than me. If they don't see the good in me, they clearly don't know what they're talking about!"

"I AM strong enough to be independent and self-sufficient."

"As a child I was told that I should never perform well before an audience. I have come to believe that the same criticism is often given in adult life. It is time to let go of this fear and follow my dreams."

"People who are successful can encourage me to achieve my goals by showing examples of how others have succeeded. Success is never possible without an abundance of examples."

"I AM confident and proud of who I am — and I AM deserving of success!"

"There are those who will suggest that there's a limit to the amount of success I can have. They might be right about some things, but they're definitely wrong about me. There is no limit to what I can accomplish."

"I am not a victim. I accept that other people will try to influence my decisions and control my life in ways that they think are good for me — but only if I let them!"

"…the world is filled with opportunities. Everything requires hard work, dedication, and patience. I am willing to commit to all of these things, so I can achieve all the success that I want!"

"I will continue on my path until I reach a place where I am completely satisfied and totally fulfilled."

"My family members, friends, and co-workers are always some of my best sources of motivation."

"I love myself so much that it gives me the confidence to take on any challenge — even if others tell me that I'm too young."

"To be successful at work, you must do whatever it takes to get the job done. If you are unfamiliar with a job, you must learn it. If you're not sure how to do something, ask someone who knows."

"I feel good when I am working on my goals, because it makes me feel free. When I worry about something that I have no control over, I feel trapped."

"Success is dependent upon perspective — the more successful other people are, the more successful I can be."

"I AM comfortable with myself for who I AM."

"One of the most important parts of my life is spending time with my family and friends. I am very lucky to have such supportive people in my life."

"I AM a good wife, mother, and friend."

"…I am a person who is well-liked and respected."

"…I AM an honest person. I always tell the truth and I never lie to someone else or myself."

"…I AM a smart person who can find solutions to the problems that I face."

"No matter what happens with my career opportunities — when I'm not getting promoted or paid more money — no one will ever be able to determine my value as a human being."

…I can have success one step at a time, so that each step leads me closer to my goals.

"I can never allow other people's mis-perceptions of me to define who I am."

"People who are successful never look upon failure as being a permanent condition."

Chapter 12:   Relationships Affirmations

Affirmations are positive statements that we say to ourselves to help us feel better about ourselves or our lives. We all have negative thoughts from time to time, but if we focus on the good in our lives, it will make us feel better. This can be especially true when it comes to our relationships. When we nurture a good relationship with ourselves and our partners, it makes us feel loved and secure.

There are many ways to use affirmations to improve your relationship with yourself and your partner. The best way is to use them as positive self-talk. This means doing positive affirmations right before you go to bed or right after you wake up, so that they become a part of your morning or evening routine. This will make the statements automatic, so that you don't even have to try thinking about them; they are already in your head as a part of your everyday routine.

In addition, you can print out these affirmations and place them on a piece of paper in your bed room. This way, when you go to bed or wake up in the morning, you'll see the affirmations and think about how they apply to your life. It's also a great idea to write down your negative thoughts on another piece of paper and then challenge those thoughts by writing down ways that negate them. Keep both pieces of paper posted in a place where you'll see them every day.

Another way to use affirmations is by writing them out on Post-It notes and placing those notes where you'll see the reminders everyday. For example, write the affirmation "I trust my partner" on a yellow Post-It note and place that note in your purse. This way, when you look down at your purse while you're walking down the street, you'll see the reminder and know it's true.

It's also great to write out negative thoughts on red Post-It notes and then write out positive counter affirmations on yellow Post-Its. So turn that negative into a positive by writing out "I love myself" on a yellow note and then writing "he loves me" on a red one. Then each time you read the red note, it will remind you of what's true.

You can also do the same thing with sticky notes and put them up in your car, in your wallet, on your computer, or in any other place where they will constantly be visible.

At first, it can be hard to catch yourself having negative thoughts and then immediately switch them into a positive affirmation. But once you get used to doing it every morning and night and seeing the reminders everywhere else throughout the day, it becomes much easier. You won't even have to try because the affirmations will become a natural way of thinking about yourself and your life.

Relationship Affirmations for Black Women:

"I am worth love."

"I am a woman of value."

"I deserve everything good in my life"

"I am an important woman to my family, friends, and partners."

"I feel good about myself today."

"I am beautiful."

"I am relaxed and calm."

"I am confident to go out in my daily life."

"I have a healthy body, psychologically and physically."

"My partner loves me unconditionally and is committed to our relationship. I accept this and see what it can bring to my life."

"My partner must know that I am supportive of him."

"He must learn to accept me as a woman, not as a black person."

"I am a good mother, daughter, sister, wife and friend."

"I have enough money to provide for my family's needs."

"I can make decisions based on what is best for me and not what others want me to do.

"I am able to make a good choice about my education, work, and other areas of my life because I know I have everything within me that I need. I accept myself as the intelligent person that I am."

"I have the inner confidence that makes me strong and able to handle anything that comes my way. No one can shake me from what's true for me, because I value myself as a woman of substance."

"I appreciate all of the love in my life, especially from those who are closest to me."

"My partner and children make me feel good about myself. They remind me how much love is in our family.

"I am a beautiful person inside and out."

"My partner loves me no matter what."

"I trust my partner to treat me well and to always be faithful to our relationship."

"The power in love is one of the strongest forms of energy on this earth. My partner, family, friends, and colleagues need all the love that they can get. They deserve it more than most people because they give it out so freely. I love them right back for what they do for me. It is my job to value them even more than they value themselves. I am the one who gives them love in return."

"My partner treats me well and I appreciate this. I do not take this generosity for granted. My partner has taught me that I deserve to be treated well, and that he thinks highly of me. We value each other and are able to have a good relationship because we have a mutual respect for the other person. This respect keeps me from feeling hurt or betrayed when my partner sometimes lets me down."

"I always have great relationships with my friends, parents, family, colleagues, and partners."

"I know what is right for myself when it comes to dating or marriage; I make the right choice based on what is best for me and my family. I know that it is possible for me to make the right choice and have a good relationship. I have self-confidence and support from my friends and family; this is why I am able to make good choices in my life."

"Others see how much value I bring to them. They know that they cannot live without me, because they need me as much as I need them."

"My friends are loyal to me. They want the best for me and do not want to hurt or betray me. This is why they are honest with me even if it means telling me something that isn't easy to hear. They know how important it is for us to be honest with each other no matter how difficult our conversations may be. They value me and they are important to me. I appreciate my friends because they make me a good person."

"I make good choices based on what is best for me. My parents and siblings support my decisions and encourage me to do the right thing."

"I am sure of what I want from life. I know exactly what I need to be happy in life. My family supports me in doing this because they also know what is best for me."

"I see good in everyone, even those who make bad choices. In this way, they can become better people. We all have a purpose on this earth and just as I do not judge someone's action when it hurts me, neither would anyone else."

"I am sure of what I want from life. I know exactly what I need to be happy in life. Others have confidence in me because they know that there is no reason for me not to succeed."

"I always have the best things in my life, and people who care about me as if they were family. My partner supports me financially and I give him all of myself in return. We are both happy together because we treat each other with respect, honor, and dignity. We are able to live happily ever after. I am sure of how I feel when it comes to the people that are closest to me; this is why I know exactly what I want from life."

"I always have a good relationship with my friends because we value each other and can be there for each other always."

"I support my family in all that they do, and they do the same for me."

"I have a great relationship with my partner. He appreciates everything I do for him and he returns the favor by being there for me as a dependable partner."

"The people closest to me have no regrets. They have accomplished everything they have set out to do in life. They come from a good place and have never done anything out of malice or anger. The people who are close to me deserve the respect that I give them because they have earned it by being good people."

"I know that successful relationships happen when both parties recognize their own needs and desires, as well as their partner's needs and desires. I can share how I feel with my partner, but they need to tell me how they feel first before knowing what's right for me. When both parties are committed to making a relationship work, it is possible to have a good relationship."

"I strive for greatness and I have confidence in myself. My problems are manageable because I understand that my only job is to be the best person I can be. I cannot let anyone or anything cause me to doubt my abilities or abilities of those who are close to me.

"I am a good mother or father. I know that my children deserve the best from me, and I try to make sure that they have it.

"The people closest to me all love each other, especially in their own unique ways. Our relationships are always solid and we are always there for each other no matter what. We laugh together, we cry together, and we understand each other's behavior because we think the same way."

"My family is well off financially. We are able to meet our needs whenever we need to go shopping or pay the bills."

"I always have a good relationship with my friends because we value each other and can be there for each other always.

"I am a good friend because I know when someone needs my help, I will be there for them unconditionally."

"I look down on those who do things that hurt others because they know that it will never be the same. The people closest to me treat me with respect, honor, and dignity. We live happily ever after because we are honest with each other and share each other's thoughts and emotions. We are able to trust each other, which is why we are able to work through our problems together."

"My partner and I share the same goals and values in life. We both like to do the same things and see eye-to-eye when it comes to how we see things in life. We communicate our feelings, goals, and dreams with each other so that we can be on the same page at all times. My partner supports me financially and I give him all of myself in return. We are both happy together because we treat each other with respect, honor, and dignity. We are able to live happily ever after."

"I have confidence that my husband knows what he wants to do with his life. He is determined to be successful and he always talks about his goals in life. He works hard and he knows how to handle himself well in all kinds of situations. I am not worried about my husband because I know that he will take care of me."

"I look down on those who do things that hurt others because they know that it will never be the same

"I am a good parent. I know that my children deserve the best from me, and I try to make sure that they have it. They are confident because they know that everything will work out in their best interest."

"I have goals and dreams for my family that I am working hard at accomplishing because I want the family to be happy."

Chapter 13:   Affirmations For Self Confidence

The black woman needs to be more confident. We need to know our worth and stop living in fear of who we are. If you need help building your confidence up, this list of affirmations is for you! Affirmations are a powerful tool for boosting your mood and can also help with personal growth as you learn to take care of yourself.

In order to build your self-confidence as a black woman, try acting as if all those things that people have been telling you about being inferior, less intelligent or less attractive don't bother you at all. These affirmations will remind you that how other people perceive us doesn't change the truth about who we really are: Women with great value and potential just waiting to be unleashed. With all that, here are some inspiring affirmations about self-confidence for black women:

"I am confident because I am powerful."

"I am powerful because I respect myself and know my value.   I value myself so much that I wear it on my sleeve!"

"I am confident because I was created in the image of God. God has designed me with a purpose, a place and an ability."

"I am confident because my ancestors were kings and queens. They overcame great obstacles with greatness."

"I am confident because being confident in myself is an act of love for myself. Being confident about myself allows me to see who God really created me to be."

"I am confident because my worth does not depend on what others say about me or how they treat me. My worth does not have a price tag on it and so no one can take it away from me. I am confident because I have a written contract with myself that says "I am worth it"!

"I am confident because I can do anything I put my mind to. When I set a goal and make the commitment to work hard, anything is possible!"

"I am confident because I can make all the wrong choices, but no one is going to take advantage of me."

"I am confident because God has great plans for my future and they don't always involve what other people say about myself. My heart will not be broken and my soul will not be meager."

"I am confident because my value can never be calculated or reduced by just one person. God always knew that I would grow and blossom. He created me for a reason. And that reason is to serve Him."

"I am confident because God's presence and love has been in my life since the beginning of time, and it is always here to stay."

"I am confident because I was part of something greater than myself: the church! It was bigger than me. And now it's bigger again!"

"I am confident because I have never felt inferior or inferiority when I stand up for myself!"

"I am confident because life is too short not to be myself. I have an awesome journey ahead of me and if I don't follow my heart, I'll miss out on it."

"I am confident because I am not a victim of circumstances or other people, but a victor of my own choices. And when I get to the end of life's journey, the only thing that can reduce my worth is if I decide to act like a victim! When others label me as less-than, it's simply their perspective. They don't know me. They don't know what God has for me. And they don't know what makes me different from everyone else. When I have a dream and I am determined to make it happen, I am confident because nothing can stand in my way."

"I am confident because there are people who care about me and they love me for me. God has given me the best family and friends, who have never let me down or misjudged me. They will always be there for me no matter what!"

"I am confident because I know that all roads don't lead to the same place. The Bible teaches us how to live our lives, how to treat others and how to think about ourselves. This is why the Bible is the most important book ever written. It's not just another book of rules, but it's a book of life! It shows me how I can do all things through Christ who strengthens me. And I know that if I allow myself to be led by my heart and completely obey God, everything will work out for the best!"

"I am confident because despite what others may say about me and whatever may happen in my life, I am safe in the arms of God. He has for me and they are not contingent on what other people say or do."

"I am confident because no matter what may happen in my life, I have a God to trust in. A Father who is bigger than any situation I can ever face. He has my back.

"I am confident because I can face those big and scary things because I know there is a bigger truth that will always be measured in all the universe. A truth that makes sense of everything."

"I am confident because I am not a slave to my circumstances or other people's perceptions. Whatever life brings me, I know it isn't going to break who God created me to be!"

"I am confident because every good and perfect gift comes from God and it's in His hands to decide when and where I will get it. And I know that it's in His hands to decide what people will think of me."

"I am confident because I have a living hope that is worth more than any amount of money."

"I am confident because God loves me and my purpose is to manifest His love to the world!"

"I am confident because there is nothing that can stop me from being who God created me to be. My confidence is rooted in the truth that God will not allow anything less."

"I am confident because my value does not depend on what others think about me, but on how well I live up to who God created me to be. "

"I am confident because I was created for a purpose. And that purpose is to honor God. And that is why I am confident!"

"I am a whole and complete person."

"I am confident."

"My worth is not determined by my success or failures, but by who I am as an individual."

"I am enough. Enough for myself. Enough for my friends. Enough for my family and my people. I am enough."

"I have choices and I have control over my life."

"I am strong, happy, and confident in every way. Whether I'm depressed or not, whether I feel like doing something or not, I choose to be happy instead."

"My life is full of positive possibilities." "I want to be optimistic about the future by expecting good things to happen while expecting bad things not to happen."

"I can be found smiling even when it's raining or when the sun is shining because I can control how I choose to feel at any given moment with my thoughts and actions. I can choose to be happy even when I am hurt or angry."

"My thoughts and actions are my own; nobody else is responsible for them."

"I am in charge of me because I want to be, not because I have to be." "I am responsible for me and no one else can make me do or think a certain way." "I've got this! I'm the only one who can talk myself out of it. Even if something terrible happens, I don't have to let it stop me from living my life the way I want it. I make it happen. My life is my own."

"My feelings are valid as they come from me and they're just as good as anyone else's feelings." "I have the right to have my feelings. I'm not trying to change them, and I don't have to take anyone's feelings over mine."

"It's perfectly fine to be angry or hurt, and I'll always feel strongly about those things. But these feelings are my own; nobody else can control them for me. I'm focused on being happy about who I am and what I do because that's the only thing that really matters to me. I'm black, I'm beautiful, and I'm so proud."

"I make my own happiness." "When people upset me, they don't change my personality or who I am. If anything it makes me more confident because it shows them how strong I am."

"I can put my needs first even if everyone else disagrees with what I'm doing."

"I love who I am and what I do for a living even though there are times when it's hard to be strong. But I'm stronger because of the people who have cared about me, loved me, and helped me through the hard times." "It will be OK and so will I. And so will you."

"Self-Affirmations for Black Women"

"I'm so much more than what you can see. I'm so much wiser than anyone could ever imagine. I don't need to be judged."

"I know who I am and that's all that matters. Nothing can change that for me because it's the truth, no matter what anyone else thinks."

"I'm not going anywhere unless it's inside my mind." "No one can make me feel different than who I am on the inside."

"I think about being happy all day long. It's what I do and it comes naturally to me. I'm in charge of my thoughts and my moods."

"I'm not going anywhere unless it's inside my mind." "No one can make me feel different than who I am on the inside."

"I don't need a reason for being happy. Happiness is just something that happens automatically when you're alive." "I'm not trying to make sense out of anything. I'm just doing what feels right inside.

"I am a black woman, and I am beautiful in every way." "Nobody has the power to make me feel any less than beautiful no matter how they see me or talk about me or treat me." "Nothing will ever change this truth about who I am and what I love about myself no matter how much anyone says otherwise. I love myself." "I am proud to be a black woman because I know that I am strong and beautiful, both inside and out."

"I will do whatever it takes to protect myself and keep my life happy." "I don't need anyone else's permission to be happy or to eat or take care of myself. I did not put this on, so I won't take it off. It's mine."

"I love myself and I don't need anyone else to tell me how to do it. I already know how to make myself happy. I've been doing it for years, and I'm going to keep doing it." "I have the power to make myself happy without anyone else's permission or approval."

"I am stronger than anyone can ever make me feel or think about myself.

"I'll feel what I need to feel, whenever that feeling hits me. But it won't stop me from doing the things I want to do. It will never stop me from being happy."

"I'm not trying to make sense out of anything. I'm just doing what feels right inside.

"I will do whatever it takes to protect myself and keep my life happy." "I don't need anyone else's permission to be happy or to eat or take care of myself. I did not put this on, so I won't take it off. It's mine."

"I am a black woman, and I love myself. And so will you." "Nothing can change that for me because it's the truth, no matter what anyone else thinks."

"I don't have to feel bad if I'm not happy." "What I think about myself and what I feel are what count. Only my thoughts and feelings matter."

"Getting upset with myself for not feeling like being happy doesn't change the truth. It only makes me more unhappy about it."

"Being upset with myself for caring about being happy doesn't change the truth either. It just feels bad no matter how hard I try to convince myself otherwise."

"I think about being happy all day long. It's what I do and it comes naturally to me. I'm in charge of my thoughts and my moods. I can be whoever I want to be, whenever I want it.

"I'm not going anywhere unless it's inside my mind." "No one can make me feel different than who I am on the inside. I'll feel what I need to feel, whenever that feeling hits me. But it won't stop me from doing the things I want to do."

"I make my own happiness."

"I love myself and so will you." "Nothing can change that for me because it's the truth, no matter what anyone else thinks.

"When people upset me they don't change my personality or who I am. If anything it makes me more confident because it shows them how strong I am."

"I have the power to make myself happy without anyone else's permission or approval. I am stronger than anyone can ever make me feel or think about myself.

"I don't have to depend on anyone else to make me happy. If it feels wrong or makes no sense for me, then that's my decision. I'll stay true to myself and do the things I like just as long as they make me happy." "I'm not trying to make sense out of anything. I'm just doing what feels right inside. "I will do whatever it takes to protect myself and keep my life happy.""

"I am a black woman, and I love myself. And so will you." "Nothing can change that for me because it's the truth, no matter what anyone else thinks."

"I don't have to be like anyone else so that I can be happy."

"Just because someone is happy doesn't mean I have to do the same things they do. Just because someone is sad doesn't mean I have to be unhappy too. Just because someone else makes me angry, it doesn't mean I have to be the same way."

Chapter 14:   Affirmations For Self-Love

A lot of things can hold you back and make you feel less confident about yourself. Sometimes, it's hard to love yourself when your insecurities are always so present and could potentially ruin your day. This list of affirmations will help you realize how powerful women are and start to love who they've been given while also giving them something that they aren't used to hearing often - self-love. These affirmations were compiled from a number of black women who experienced some form of discrimination or violence based on their race, gender, appearance, and sexual orientation during their lives on this planet Earth. To help empower you, they made a list of affirmations that they would have liked to hear growing up to remind them that they were still beautiful and lovable regardless of what society has sown.

"I'm who I am"

"There's nothing wrong with my body, it's the way it was created by God for me to be full of strength and beauty"

"Being black isn't all bad, there are lots of things that are positive about being black: strong, powerful, confident, and most of all brave; just like I am!   "

"I'm strong, I'm confident, I'm beautiful and I'm brave!"

"I accept myself completely"

"There's hope for your future: you can overcome obstacles, lose weight and love yourself no matter what!" "You're unique and beautiful exactly as you are!"

"Don't let fear stop you from doing things or saying things that you want to do or say. Be bold! Be brave! Be a leader!

Black women are often taught that they should stay quiet when they have something to say because it will make them sound stupid. But the truth is, there's nothing wrong with being confident and being able to express yourself. There are no barriers to your success as a woman if you believe in yourself, but you have to be willing to put in the hard work to achieve it."

"After all these years of being told I'm not good enough or beautiful enough and hearing other women tell me that I'm not pretty enough and that I look like a boy, I want to shout "THOSE ARE MY WORDS!!""

"I deserve respect and kindness from the world. No one has ever been kind or respectful of me or my culture. No one has ever respected me. No one has ever loved me. I am all alone in the world and there's nothing anyone can do to change this. People will always order me to sit down and stay quiet, ignore me when I try to tell them how they can help me, or attack my ideas and walk over me just because they don't like them."

"You are not a failure because you were born with dark skin"

"I've been told I'm strong when I wanted to give up on everything. I've been told that God has blessed me when I wanted to stop believing. I've been called a smart girl, when I wanted to give up on school. I've been called a beautiful girl, when I wanted to stop wearing makeup. I've been told that God came to me in prayer, when I wanted to run away from Him."

"It's not my body that's ugly just because it doesn't look like theirs! It's how they percieved my body that is ugly!"

"I'm the strongest and most powerful woman in the world and no one can tell me otherwise."

"You are beautiful! You are intelligent! You are kind! You are humble! You're bold and you're brave. You're everything that other people call your flaws. You are perfect just the way you are!"

"You are beautiful and so are you. You're unique and precious, and everyone should love you."

"There's nothing wrong with me. I'm not crazy because I get jealous about what others have. There's nothing wrong with me getting upset about people making fun of me or treating me bad because it doesn't make me crazy- I'm just hurting."

"I am beautiful inside and out. I'm intelligent. I have a good heart. I have strong morals and values. Knowing this only makes me more proud to be black."

"You're not stupid for being different about your hair or your clothes or what sex you happen to be or anything else that's unique about you. You're not less of a woman because you like anime, or for liking different kinds of music or for dressing in an unusual way. You're stronger, you're smarter and you can do whatever it is you choose to do."

"I know what's best for me. No one can tell me how to live my life except for myself."

"I'm not going to stop loving who I am just because someone else says I don't deserve to love myself and others should hate me too. They're the ones who need help not me. They're the ones who aren't happy with themselves or their lives."

"No matter what anyone says or does, I deserve love and kindness from everyone in this world. That is all that matters. Always. I am the most important person on this earth, and I am entitled to be treated that way."

"The only person I need ever be concerned with is me. I'll never hurt anyone else no matter what they think of me. They can try to tear me down but they can't tear down who I truly am as a person."

"I'm not addicted to any 'bad' things anymore. I've made myself stronger and smarter, like my mom always said."

"I can do anything because I believe in myself and in the people around me who believe in me as well."

"I'm special because everyone has their own unique gifts and talents but what makes me unique is that I know how to find my inner peace and appreciate everything around me no matter what happens. I know how to move on from things in my past and look for a brighter future."

"I'm special because I've been through hell and come out on the other side to lead a happy, successful life just as anyone else can."

"Everyone deserves to be treated with respect, kindness, compassion and love. Everyone deserves that special someone who will treat them like the special person they really are. Everyone deserves happiness no matter what their race or culture is."

"I'm not pretending everything is perfect all of the time – but I'm going to make myself better when everything around me keeps making me feel bad. I hope everyone can do this too."

"I won't limit myself because society tells me so. I'll never be able to do everything everyone else can, but I will always try my best and get the most out of life. I won't let myself be limited by what anyone else says about me, or how they look or treat me."

"I don't want anyone to tell me who I am or what I should do with my life. No one in this world has the right to make that choice for me, unless it makes them happy. That person is not happy for you and only cares about themselves."

"I'm a strong and smart woman who's survived against all odds and I'm not going to stop fighting for what it's worth until everyone on this earth is treated like equal human beings. As long as I exist, I will fight to make sure that no one in this world is treated like a second class citizen."

"I want everyone to know that their life matters, no matter what anyone says. I want people to love themselves and know that it's okay to be who they are and lead a healthy, happy life."

"I'm not going to let anyone manipulate me or use me. I deserve this respect from everyone in my life because it's taken me years to learn how to stand up for myself and others."

"No one can tear me down just because they have something against me. They don't have the right to tell other people that I'm a bad person and shouldn't be treated as well as everyone else. Just because someone has something against me, doesn't make it okay for them to treat me poorly."

"I don't need anyone's approval for who I am or how I live my life, but if I do get it then it's always nice to hear. If someone truly thinks that you're a horrible person, then you don't need them in your life anyway. You can live without their opinion. You can live without their love and support. You're better off that way."

"I have no reason to continue to be with someone who doesn't treat me well. There's no one in this world who would want to be treated poorly, so I will make sure they understand that they're dealing with a strong, independent and confident woman who won't take their crap anymore. They can make themselves happy without me."

"No one could ever hurt or hate me unless I let them — and I won't! Ever! They couldn't if they tried."

"I'm a good mother and friend, just by being myself. If anyone tells you otherwise then know that you don't need them around in your life. You are enough just by being yourself and if you continue to love and respect yourself, no one can ever say anything to make you question your value."

"I believe in myself because I've never doubted myself over the years because of what some other people say about me when I'm not even around them. I'll never make excuses for the way I live my life. I have to respect myself and I have to love myself before anyone else will."

> "Even if everyone else makes you feel inferior, out of place, stupid or not good enough — your family will always love and accept you for who you are. Even if your friends abandon you or betray your trust — family is always there to support and protect you. You just have to acknowledge them first."

"I am special. Everyone around me is special in their own way. Everyone in this world is looking for their peace and happiness. I will make myself happy no matter what others tell me."

"I don't need everyone to love me or think I'm a good person, but it's nice when someone admits they care about me. It means a lot when someone can find a way to love me despite all of my flaws."

"No matter how bad things may get in my life — there will never be a time when I am too broken down that my family and friends cannot help me up again and help restore my faith in humanity."

"No one deserves any less respect than anyone else because they are not the same race, nationality or gender as you. Even if someone does something wrong, you should never give up on them because everyone deserves the chance to make their dreams come true."

"I will love myself and treat myself with the respect that I deserve. I know that I may have made mistakes in my life, but that doesn't mean they can make me feel bad forever. No one can ever tell me who I am or what I'm worth."

"No one knows what someone else is going through or why they do certain things. You can never judge another person for their actions until you've walked a mile in their shoes."

"I will love my life and live it to the fullest no matter how many people tell me otherwise. I will never allow anyone to make me feel like I should be doing something more with my life. I will always follow my heart."

"I am not a second class citizen, a bad person, or a lowlife because of what some other people might think of me. I will always be proud of myself because I know who I am and what I deserve. I will never allow them to take my happiness away."

"You don't need anyone's permission to be a better person than they are. You don't have to make them like you or respect you in order for them to deserve the same treatment."

"Love and kindness comes from within and no one can ever eradicate your happiness if you only love yourself. Love means caring, accepting and respecting someone else regardless of their flaws. You should never expect someone else to act any different than they do. It's always nice when someone says that you're special, but it's even nicer when they tell you how special you really are. I will continue to love myself and make myself happy no matter what anyone else thinks or says about me."

"I won't allow anyone to discourage me from being my best self. I can't afford to let other people make me feel inadequate in any way, shape or form. It's better for everyone if I do what I feel is right with my life instead of listening to them."

"No one is ever going change the person that you are or the choices you make. It's best if you stay true to yourself and live with the choices you make."

"I will love myself as much as I'll allow others to love me. In return, I will treat myself with the respect I deserve. If other people won't respect or love me, then they're not worth my time or attention."

"I will never betray my principles because I know what kind of person I deserve to be. No one can change who I am – but the way that I live my life can change who other people are. The more that others respect and accept me for who I am, the happier and better off I will be in life. I will never allow anyone to tell me that I'm not good enough. I can only be what I am and if people don't respect me for it then they're not worth my friendship."

"No matter what kind of life someone has lived in the past, they deserve a second chance. You should never judge a book by its cover."

"I know that there will always be someone who is bigger or better than you are, but that doesn't mean you have to feel inferior to them. You can have your own sense of pride and self-worth without comparing yourself to someone else just because they are different than you. I will always keep in mind that there are more important things to worry about than other people."

"No matter how many people you think are better than you, don't ever doubt your own self-worth. You have the right to be who you want to be in life. That right shouldn't be taken away from you just because someone doesn't understand your sense of purpose in this world or the way that you live your life."

"Even if my family may not always understand me and my choices, they can still accept me for who I am and love me unconditionally. It's best if I surround myself with understanding people who can show me that everyone deserves a second chance no matter what they've done in their past. I will never allow anyone to hold me down and make me feel bad about the decisions I've made in my life. I will find a way to love myself so that others can love me too."

"I will always keep in mind that no matter how much my life can change, I am always going to be the same person I was when it begins. It's better to look at the good things in life instead of the bad because you never know which one is going to come around again someday."

"While other people are constantly trying to change who you are, you should only try for yourself. You don't need anyone else's permission or approval to be happy and successful.

"I will never allow anyone to change who I am or the choices that I make in life. You have to have your own principles, morals and standards in order to be happy in your own skin. No one can change that about you – only yourself."

"You don't need anyone's permission to be who you want to be or get what you want out of life. If someone is unwilling to accept your values and do things their way, then they aren't good enough for your life anyway."

"Even if people don't like what you do or how you live your life, you should never give them the satisfaction of changing for them. You don't need anyone else's permission to be who you are or achieve your goals. You can only be who you are – no matter what other people say about you." "I will not allow someone else to tell me where I should be in life or how my future should turn out. I am the only one who can tell me what my future should be like and how to live it. I will never allow someone else to make me feel inadequate or worthless in any way, shape or form."

"I've realized that you don't have to change for anyone else, you just need to change for yourself in order to be happy. No one can ever take away your happiness if you only love yourself. Happiness is something that no one else can ever give you – only you can give it back to yourself."

"There's nothing wrong with going at your own pace and living a life filled with fun, meaning and purpose. You don't need anyone's permission in order to be happy. It's your right to be satisfied and proud of what you have accomplished. You don't have to change for anyone else – but if you're content with who and how you live your life, that's something that no one can ever take away from you."

"You should never let the opinions of others make you feel inferior or waste your time on other people. They might laugh at the things you do or say, but they'll never laugh at how good it feels to be yourself."

"You shouldn't let someone else's standards for who you should be determine how good of a person you are. You are who you are and that's all that matters. You shouldn't let anyone or anything else get in your way of seeing yourself the way that you really are."

"If you try to be anyone other than yourself, then there will always be something missing from your life. No matter what other people say, you should never doubt the kind of person that you really are deep down inside."

"Even if other people try their best to change your opinion about yourself, don't give them any satisfaction of succeeding in it. They can never make you feel unworthy just because they think differently than you do. You don't have to change for anyone else – especially if you're happy in your own skin."

"Even if others make fun of you for being yourself, that doesn't mean you should ever change for them. You don't have to try and be someone else. People can mock and laugh at you all they want – but that's their problem, not yours." "If someone tries to change who you are or what you do, just because it's not how THEY would do things… Don't let them take away your individuality.

"If someone tries to make you feel like you're worthless or unable to do things the way that you want, then don't ever let them convince you that that's what you are. You are who you are and that is all there is to it. You don't have to try and be someone else." "Even if the people in your life criticize your choices, they shouldn't ever tell you how to live your life. You should let them know how happy they'll be when they stop trying to change who you truly are."

"You shouldn't let other people constantly try and make changes in your life if it's not what YOU want. It's okay to not want to be like everyone else and make your own choices. You need to live the life that's right for you."

"Sometimes people will try and change who you are because they don't think you will make it in life. Don't take their advice if they don't believe in you."

"You should never feel the need to change who you are because of what someone else thinks of you. Don't accept any of the negative criticism that is directed toward you just because someone doesn't like how happy you are with yourself."

"No matter how many times people try to knock you down, YOU have the final word on whether or not that bothers YOU. Don't let others bring you down. You can't please everyone, so don't ever try."

"You are only responsible for yourself and you shouldn't ever let anyone make you feel like your life is not good enough. You can't please everyone, so some people might think badly of you just because they don't approve of who YOU are."

"You should never try to be someone else or live a different kind of life just to get the approval or acceptance of others. You should accept yourself first and foremost – and if other people have a problem with that, then that's their problem, not yours. Don't change for anyone else."

"There's nothing wrong with being different and not trying to be like everyone else. You are supposed to be who YOU want to be, not someone else. Be proud of who you are and don't ever let anyone make you feel bad about yourself."

"You should never try to change your personality or the way that you live just because someone doesn't like how it makes them feel. You have to do whatever makes you the happiest person in the world."

Chapter 15: Affirmations For Self-Control

Having the will power to win in a relationship can take dedication and practice. Many times, black women are let down in relationships because they cannot control their emotions or impulses. It is important to work on both self-control and patience. This list of self-control affirmations for female black people is invaluable in your quest to stay patient with your partner, or reminding yourself that you are strong enough to make choices when the going gets tough. These affirmations will help curb impulse control problems such as feelings of frustration, anger, irritability, impatience, impulsiveness and a short fuse.

This is a list of affirmations to use when you find yourself in a situation where you are concerned about your self-control. Some of these may be applied for short-term situations, but others should be more permanent reminders to yourself. Re-reading the self control affirmations when your patience has dwindled will help reinforce your ability to make the necessary changes in your behavior.

The self-control affirmations for black women on this page can help you to refocus and keep it together with patience, especially if you are feeling like you are about to lose control. Whenever life gets hard, just remember how strong you really are and how much better life will be if you keep it all together. If a certain situation is causing you to lose control, try saying the affirmation repeatedly until you calm down or reach your destination and can no longer be a part of the situation. The last thing you want to do is lose control in public, so be sure to watch yourself and keep it all together no matter how hard life gets.

List of Self-Control Affirmations for Black Women

Self-Control Affirmations

"I have the self control that God gave me I have the self control that God gave me"

"I know my own strength; I am empowered to get over anything that stands in my way"

"I have the self control that God gave me"

"I am a young woman of power, and I do not allow anyone to take advantage of me"

"I can pick myself up when life knocks me down... And I will never give up."

"I let my anger be a red flag to show me when I'm at risk. Then I take a deep breath, let go of it and feel better,"

"I have the self-control to get through any problem without letting it get me down"

"If something gets on my nerves, I can avoid getting angry by using sound reasoning."

"I choose health over junk food; I am not powerless against my desires."

"The fear of feeling ashamed is greater than my craving for that sweet treat."

"I deserve the time I spend doing something productive. I will take the time to enjoy my hobbies and build better habits."

"I am strong enough to resist negative thoughts and feelings, even when I'm feeling vulnerable."

"I am not at fault for everything that goes wrong in my life; I am just as capable of achieving success as any other person."

"I will continue to make wise decisions every day of my life, even when I just want a little break from reality. "

"I choose hard work over no work. I will not depend on others to take care of me."

"I love myself and deserve good things, even when I am struggling with a bad habit."

"I am exceptionally talented, capable and successful; I have a lot to offer the world."

"I have access to knowledge and resources of the highest caliber."

"The reward I seek is in my heart.

"If people didn't want to be around me because of who I was, they wouldn't be doing so now."
"People are not worthy of a second chance at betterment. "

"I am responsible for my own happiness."

"I am not driven by negativity or toxic emotions."

 "I am not driven by addiction or negative feelings."

"I am not committed to short term pleasure."

"I no longer focus on how I've been mistreated in the past."

"Hurtful experiences from my past do not dictate my future."

"I can recognize and pursue my interests, even if they are different from the expectations of others."

 "Today I see myself acting in a self-controlled way."

"I am not controlled by addictions."

"I am a strong and capable woman who can overcome my negative emotions and choose good instead."

"The world does not revolve around me."

"I am stronger than I give myself credit for"

"I have the power within me to change my emotions whenever I choose and create _____ (whatever you want).

"I will not allow this to get the best of me."

"I refuse to be defined by this."

"I AM MORE THAN THIS!"

"Your opinion of me is not what my reality is."

"No one can make you feel inferior without your consent."

Chapter 16:   Affirmations for Self-Esteem

The need for self-esteem among black women is rarely discussed, yet it's one of the most important things to have in order to live your best life. Self-esteem affects everything from how we feel about our bodies, what our next steps are in life and relationships, and more.

Below you'll find a list of affirmations which will help you build up your self-esteem so that you can live your best life!

"I am unique"

"I am on the right path"

"Today will be great"

"I am beautiful the way I am"

"Everything is going to work out for me tomorrow, and I'm meant to do great things in this world."

"I look forward to my future, and I'm excited about it." Self-Esteem Affirmations

"I am my own person with my own unique strengths, flaws and abilities."

"I am deserving. "

"I am confident."

"I have abundant resources."

" I am informed. I know what I need to do now. And I will do it. "

"I am deserving."

"I am confident."

"I am strong. I can handle what comes my way."

"My self-worth is not dependent on any particular outcome or person – neither positive nor negative. I love myself no matter what."

"I am worthy."

"I am gorgeous."

"I love myself."

" I know I'm important."

" I am strong ."

" I am confident ."

" I am intelligent."

"I have a complete understanding of myself and the world around me."

"I am successful wherever I go."

"I have a right to be here, and I deserve to be here."   "I belong."

" I am beautiful ."

"I embrace who I am."

"My worth is not dependent on my race, gender, class, sexual orientation or any other factor. It is inherent, inherent in my being and intrinsic to who I am. My value transcends time and space. And it is limitless. I love my whole self."

"I embrace who I am."

"I am confident ." "I'm good at what I do. I make a difference. And I'm successful."

"I am beautiful ."

"I appreciate the beauty that is within me, and I can be proud of myself for it. The process of reflecting on the gifts of life is one of the most powerful avenues for self-love that we can take part in."

"My worth is not dependent on any factor, including race, gender, class or sexual orientation. My worth lies within me – inside my soul – and it is unlimited. I love my whole self."

"I am beautiful."

" I am a feminist ."

"I know I'm important, and that I have a purpose."

"I have a complete understanding of myself and the world around me."

"Everyone has value, regardless of race or gender. My worth is not dependent on any factor, including race, gender, class or sexual orientation. My worth lies within me – inside my soul – and it is unlimited. I love my whole self. "

"I love myself "

" I deserve to be here. And I belong ."   "I'm good at what I do. I make a difference. And I'm successful ."

Conclusion

Thank you for listening all the way to the end; keep repeating these affirmations because this book will help you feel great for the rest of your life.

Positive affirmations are powerful, but when you're a Black woman, they're much more so. Many Black women have the ability to succeed in their careers, but they frequently allow fear or lack of confidence stand in their way. This is where affirmations may help! Without any outside support, affirmations give you the power to shift your thinking and start believing in yourself! This blog will discuss how negative beliefs effect us, why self-affirmations are so important for Black women, and positive affirmation examples for Black women.

Many of us, whether consciously or subconsciously, hold negative views about ourselves. Some of these thoughts are particular to our current situation, such as "I don't have enough money" and "I won't receive that promotion." Some negative ideas, such as "Black women are not as successful as white women," or "I should be smarter than everyone else," are more widespread. Negative beliefs might make you feel depressed or insufficient.

When we have unfavorable self-perceptions, our emotions will reflect that. That is why our thoughts have such a strong influence on our emotions. Your self-esteem will be harmed if you believe you are less valued than others or that you are not smart enough to reach your goals. Your mood will improve if you believe you are valued and intelligent, on the other hand! This is especially true for Black women!

Negative self-perceptions can influence how others perceive you. When people criticize you or make assumptions about who you are and what success means to you, you may overreact or tear yourself down. Rather of confronting these circumstances head on, you may begin to doubt yourself and your ability.

You may feel fatigued or even fall ill as a result of this. You'll begin to believe that there is nothing nice in the world, and this will have an impact on every aspect of your life! Starting with how you see yourself and then how others see you, your confidence, happiness, and even your health can all be affected. That is why it is critical for Black women to use positive affirmations about themselves!

The first step in modifying negative self-perceptions is to recognize them when they arise. If you're always feeling like a failure, for example, you can consider what thoughts or feelings are creating this. If you continually believe that your ethnicity makes you less valuable than white people or that your gender makes it hard for you to succeed at work, it's time to change your mind.

After you've identified the issue, take a step back and consider how negative ideas might effect your life. Are they making you nervous? Are they causing you to become ill? By putting down the evidence for and against these ideas, you can put them to the test. Consider how other Black women have achieved success if you're having doubts about yourself due of your color. They may have had to work harder than white folks, but they were nonetheless successful!

It takes time to overcome a negative self-perception. Don't give up if it takes a long time. The more positive affirmations for Black women you practice and repeat, the more likely you are to believe them! They will gradually replace the negative thoughts that are preventing you from achieving success and pleasure!

It's crucial to maintain these affirmations for Black women on hand at all times so that you may use them whenever you need them.

The planet is constantly in motion. People are getting sicker and sicker. Conflicts are intensifying. The world is becoming more and more arid. It's normal if you're feeling bewildered, weary, or restless with so much going on. "Hang in there," I encourage you, "all will turn out OK."

Positive affirmations can help you change the way your mind thinks. You may learn to control how you see, react to, and process information and events in your life. Positive affirmations can also assist you in realizing your full potential and achieving better success. Believe in yourself and your ability, and you'll see speedy results.

You can converse with this book as if it were a pal. Keep it on your person at all times. When you're terrified, upset, or lost, it's a good idea to consult it. Reconnect with your inner strength. Rest and re-energize yourself. And you'll have a renewed feeling of purpose and determination for tomorrow. Because your life is a vital contribution to the world, live it with hope, love, and kindness.

Made in the USA
Columbia, SC
25 February 2022

56834865R00072